# SOUL ON SOUL CONTACT

*Face your T.R.U.T.H.S. head on*

By,

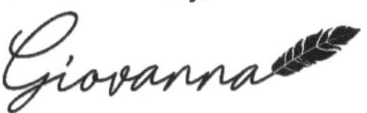

*T.R.U.T.H.S*

*Trials reveal understanding through healing self*

#TRUTHS

## Where to connect

Signs of Empowerment LLC
www.signsofempowerment.com

FB page: Signs of Empowerment
IG page: @signsofempowerment

My Personal account
IG page: @Iam.possible212

© 2018 Giovanna Pryor Signs of Empowerment LLC

*All rights reserved. No part of this book may be used or reproduced in any manner whatsoever without the written permission from the author. No part of this book may be used or reproduced by any means, graphic, electronic, or mechanical, including photocopying, recording, taping or by any information storage retrieval system without the written permission of the publisher except in the case of brief quotations embodied in critical articles and reviews.*

The author of this book does not dispense medical advice or prescribe the use of any technique as a form of treatment for physical, emotional, or medical problems. The reader should regularly consult a physician in matters relating to his/her health and particularly concerning any symptoms that may require diagnosis or medical attention. The intent of the author is only to offer information of a general nature to help you in your quest for emotional and spiritual well-being. In the event you use any of the information in this book for yourself, which is your constitutional right, the author and the publisher assume no responsibility for your actions.

*(Health, alternative healing)*

All photos throughout the book were taken by Giovanna Pryor
Cover designed by **pro_ebookcovers** using Giovanna Pryor's personal photo and stock imagery by flicker.com

SECOND EDITION

Signs of Empowerment LLC rev date: 1/1/2019

11:11

Use this book as a beacon of hope,
a missing piece to your puzzle.
Creating a roadmap as we go along.
Remember, life is a journey, not a destination,
getting lost is just part of the adventure.
Once you learn balance,
you will be able to ride the waves of life.

\* \* \*

I dedicate this book to YOU!
I wrote this, in hopes we could connect.

*There will be many books in the series SOUL ON SOUL CONTACT,
and an audio book of this available soon.
This is only the beginning chapters of my journey
writing to the Universe.*

I'd like to thank my husband, who is also my best friend,
for being my biggest support system.
I know I haven't always been easy to deal with, especially during my
low points, but you never gave up on me or stopped loving me.
I am so grateful for you and our family.

I'd also like to thank my past for my artistic inspiration.
If I had not struggled during my lowest point,
I would have never known my true strength.
You helped awaken my inner lioness.

*This is an easy read, written to tease your thinking,
grab your interest and empower yourself to heal.
Grab a notebook and pen, it is time to get vulnerable.*

I pray you feel the encouragement through this book.
May you receive healing, strength from your own self-discovery.
I pray that you begin to feel empowered as you start
to overcome your fears,
by re-learning and remembering you have the power within
to unlock all your mental chains!
I love you!

## Table of Contents

Soul on soul contact .................................................................. 1
Chapter 1
  Soul contract ........................................................................... 9
Chapter 2
  Formal introduction ............................................................. 12
Chapter 3
  Walk with me ........................................................................ 14
Chapter 4
  This is me ............................................................................... 16
Chapter 5
  Tales of her love affair ......................................................... 20
Chapter 6
  Letting go, to gain ................................................................. 22
Chapter 7
  It's time, there's a shift ........................................................ 31
Chapter 8
  The antidote for our INTERNAL pain ................................ 33
Chapter 9
  T.R.U.T.H.S OR DARE ........................................................... 36
Chapter 10
  Befriending the beast .......................................................... 39
Chapter 11
  Trusting the process ............................................................ 46
Chapter 12
  Who are you? ........................................................................ 50
Chapter 13
  You must break, in order to heal ....................................... 54
Chapter 14
  Your pain has a purpose ...................................................... 58
Chapter 15
  Building up self ..................................................................... 61
Chapter 16
  I am .......................................................................................... 63
Chapter 17
  You are what you eat ........................................................... 69
Chapter 18
  Dear younger self ................................................................. 72
Chapter 19
  Frozen in fear ........................................................................ 76
Chapter 20
  When the enemy is you ...................................................... 79
Chapter 21
  Silently trying to starve out my imperfections .............. 82
Chapter 22
  Let's start a conversation ................................................... 86
Chapter 23
  Message received ................................................................ 91

Chapter 24
Why?......................................................................................................... 95
Chapter 25
Mirage, Playing catch up....................................................................... 98
Chapter 26
Releasing and forgiveness.................................................................. 102
Chapter 27
Law of attraction ................................................................................. 105
Chapter 28
Be you without making excuses ....................................................... 109
Chapter 29
Self-love, eating organically .............................................................. 111
Chapter 30
Becoming me........................................................................................ 113
Chapter 31
When your wings arrive ..................................................................... 117
Chapter 32
Relationships........................................................................................ 122
Chapter 33
Soul food............................................................................................... 127
Chapter 34
Becoming your own superhero ........................................................ 130
Chapter 35
It's time, so start getting ready!........................................................ 133
Chapter 36
Feel empowered, not powerless ...................................................... 135
Chapter 37
Do you really need eyes to see?....................................................... 138
Chapter 38
Stepping into your own purpose ...................................................... 140
Chapter 39
Affirm your greatness ........................................................................ 142
Chapter 40
Confirmation of payment .................................................................. 145
Chapter 41
Flipbook the process .......................................................................... 148
Chapter 42
Messages to my soul tribe ................................................................. 155
Chapter 43
Notes to self ......................................................................................... 160
Chapter 44
Quick tips .............................................................................................. 164
Chapter 45
It's never goodbye it's only, see you later...................................... 169

# CHAPTER 1

## *Soul contract*

> *"Unlock your understanding,*
> *and you will reveal your healing."*
> *-Giovanna*

This is a self-empowerment book written to the Universe,
for the Universe with you, in mind.
I have been looking forward
to this Divine connection.

Here I am by the book,
as an open book.

Transparent and vulnerable.
I bare it all to you.
I share with you
My T.R.U.T.H.S.
in all faithfulness.

I am buried deep within this book,
as it has been buried deep within me.

As you uncover my truths,
you will start to recognize your own.

The reflection will reveal itself.

        **T. Trials**
        **R. Reveal**
   **U. Understanding**
     **T. Towards**
     **H. Healing**
        **S. Self**
       **#TRUTHS**

I share MY T.R.U.T.H.S so you
may see my trials and
understand the connection.

Empowering you,
to write
your own
T.R.U.T.H.S

*11:11*

*Signs of Empowerment*

---

*It is time, to liberate your soul with your own T.R.U.T.H.S,
and light the way through the darkness.*

---

**I understand the power of struggle,
I understand the power of sacrifice,
I even understand the power of pain.**

**All because I've been there,
I've lived it,
I've felt it,
and I've made it out alive.**

*I see now that my struggles brought out the best in me,
my sacrifices made me see the beauty in life,
and my pain revealed my true strength.*

---

*Only, through understanding and forgiveness,
can we ever understand ourselves, and attempt, to love again.*

---

***I found my understanding, from my experiences,
my compassion, from my pain,
and wisdom, from my darkness.***

Let me reveal myself to you,
showing you my unfiltered,
broken, and most intimate self.
How deep and honest
will you get with yourself?

*\*\*Close your eyes and take a deep breath\*\**

We are entering a place of vulnerability,
a judgment free zone

Protected by the Divine,
let us go within.

Allow yourself to become vulnerable, don't hold back now.
It's time to start to heal our souls.

Let's start with gratitude,
I am grateful to be alive
I am grateful for the fresh air that I breathe
I am grateful for the roof over my head
I am grateful for the foods I eat and the nourishment it gives my body
I am grateful for the jobs that I have and the income I make
I am grateful I am aligned and living in my purpose.

Now, let's Affirm

I am powerful
I am learning
I am growing
I am healing
I am allowing the spirit to flow through me
I let go of my pain
I let go of my heartache
I let go of my resentment
I allow myself to grow into who I am meant to become,
no longer holding myself back.

This book is filled with sweet treats, and hidden delights. quotes, poems, gratitude's, and affirmations with teases of what is in store for the books to come. Some of my writing throughout this book is from when I was younger, going through the struggles, combined with the lessons I've learned after. Woven and completed with the empowerment that I've gained along the way.

I pray you enjoy this book, as much as I enjoyed writing it.
**I already feel the connection.**
May it jump start your journey to internal healing.
Shall we begin?

# CHAPTER 2

## *Formal introduction*

Hi there!
So Nice to meet you!
My name is **Giovanna**

This wasn't by
**Coincidence** that
we are meeting,
and it's not by **chance**
that you are reading this.

*Photo edited using photolab app*

"Everything happens for a reason"
my grandma always said that, and it's tatted on my back,
because *I truly believe that!*

*I am covered in ink, messages, and signs to myself.*
*A collection of the chapters I have lived through, and*
*the strength I needed to survive.*

So, call this **divine intervention,**
don't worry you're not in trouble,
**you've been asking for** this,
for **healing and answers,**
you've sent up your prayers.

11:11
Are you tuned in?
Do I have your attention?

*Can you hear my voice?*
*Do you feel my spirit?*
*Don't worry, you're not crazy.*
I come in Peace,

with Love and Light.
On a mission,
to heal the world,
one soul, at a time.

I am your friendly tour guide,
here to re-introduce you to your own soul :)

*Soul on Soul contact,*
*this is what you have asked for,*
*I know you've been yearning for me,*
*don't be shy now...*
*What? Am I too good to be true?*

*Don't get this confused,*
*Look in the mirror; I am really you.*

Throughout this book, I will be like your personal, guardian angel.
helping you relearn how to hear and trust your own intuition,
find your voice,
control your own thoughts,
and reconnect with the Divine within you.

*Crazy right?!*
*Just a little bit,*
*but aren't we all a little crazy?*
*So, let's talk.*

# CHAPTER 3

## *Walk with me*

> *"I have healing in my purpose,*
> *and wisdom in my soul,*
> *but I had lost my voice to speak."*
> *-Giovanna*

I was broken alone in my darkness,
scared of my own light.

But this is my life's purpose,
and I am here taking center stage.
It is time.

My voice needs to be heard,
my love needs to be felt!
A connection needs to be made!


>I am on a universal mission,
>to help aid, in the process of healing the world.
>You will remember my words,
>they will bring comfort, healing,
>and love to all, filled with gained wisdom and pain.
>They will live on for generations to come.
>As I grow, so will my writing.
>As I expand, so will my words.
>
>I've been hiding in fear,
>fear of being my raw, authentic self.
>But here I am!
>
>Leading by example
>baring it all,
>in front of the entire world.
>
>In hopes, you will do the same.
>These are my T.R.U.T.H.S.
>Here are my scars
>Look at my reflection.

*Let's make a deeper Connection,
let's vibe on a spiritual level
Soul on Soul Contact*

Does Your soul crave something deeper and more intimate?
Vulnerable yet playful?

*Do you seek a deeper understanding of yourself?*

I am what you have been seeking
I am you.

And I have a message.

# CHAPTER 4

## *This is me*

*"The liberation that words can create,
can bring instant freedom to your soul and spirit.
Use that pen and notebook and redirect your life."
-Giovanna*

I have a passion for writing, Evernote© was my sanctuary during my struggles in my 20s.

I've had this, and many other books in my spirit, and buried deep within my soul.

But I have been trapped in my own fears, scared of speaking my own truths, trying desperately to find my voice.

*I had to do my own healing first,
blood, sweat, and tears,
both internally and externally, spiritually and mentally.
I can't lie it's been rough, filled with up's and downs,
winning and losing, smiles and tears,
pain and growth, breaking and healing.
It's taken longer than I expected,
but deep down I know I am exactly on time
11.11*

I can't even begin to tell you the struggle mentally it was for me to complete this.
**Fear of your own power and purpose is real!**

*You may lose people, but stay focused,*
*you will gain yourself, and that is priceless.*

I did a lot of questioning, mixed with A LOT of excuses
and then I did the hardest thing imaginable,
I started to face my own ugly T.R.U.T.H.S. uncovering the fact,
My biggest FEAR was;
I was SCARED of my OWN REFLECTION.

How can you defeat a villain you are too scared to face?
I know, it can be terrifying facing your greatest enemy,
the reflection in the mirror, yourself.
It has been for me!

> Nearly all of my life,
> I have been fighting a battle
> against myself.

Then, finally, 6 or 7 years ago disease manifested, and my whole
body began fighting against itself autoimmune style.
*(I was later diagnosed with positive ANA and told I had Lupus)*

I couldn't hide it anymore,
I couldn't ignore it.
**It was time to learn how to fight back,**
And remember how to heal!

> "I am a warrior almost defeated at my own war.
> Here to share the wisdom,
> I gained on the mental battlefield."
> -Giovanna

Let me show you how
I learned how to feed my own soul.

I suggest getting your own notebook,
so you can start exploring your T.R.U.T.H.S,
make notes, there will be different tasks you will be asked
to do called Note Time. Such as writing your own affirmations,
starting a gratitude journal and much more.

*Let's start to rewrite your old mind games,*

*and get a catchy self-love song stuck in your head.*

Do you seek a deeper understanding of yourself?

Do you feel a connection with the Universe?

Do you talk to Spirit? (God/Source)

Have you ever talked to your soul?

Did you know you had one?

I am what you have been seeking,
I am you.
We've never been formally introduced.
I have a message

-your higher self

*The liberation that words can create,
can bring instant freedom to your soul and spirit.
Use that pen and notebook.*

When, you are having a terrible day or just in a mood.
Grab a pen and paper and start to write out the future *how* you want to see. Describe what you see, how you feel, even what you smell, and write your own fairy tale. Change your thinking, expand your mind, and live out your dreams, it is possible.

Read out loud these affirmations, with belief, and power, smile,
and feel the feelings that you are affirming.

I am grateful, I am happy, I am healthy, I am strong, I am supported,
I am determined, I am worthy, I am blessed, I am successful, I am
abundant, I am loved, I am respected, I am determined, I am appreciated, I am surrounded by love, and I am protected by 1,000 angels.

All is well.

*Notebook Time:*

*Now is the time to write you're your own affirmations.*

*Write out on paper and affirm out loud with belief and power.*

*To build your spiritual muscles even more,*
*continue daily in front of the mirror, until and even after,*
*desired results.*

# CHAPTER 5

## Tales of her love affair

*"Getting intimate with self, is a process,
it is accepting your vulnerability,
and embracing the gift of self."*
*-Giovanna*

Falling in love with myself,
was the most illuminating experience that has ever happened to me.
Loving myself so passionately, that I craved my own energy, was a feeling
I never felt before.
I am fascinated by my own spirit, as I recognize,
we are all an embodiment of the Divine.
Let me give you a taste of my love notes to self.
When I was first meeting, and falling in love with myself,
it was love at first sight, it was pure bliss that I could not hide.
Just a warning it is highly addictive
and will change your life forever.

---

With a pen and paper in hand, her heart and soul poured out.
Bleeding on the pages was the pain she had bottled up.

---

She was bursting at the seams.
The tears began to flow,

the words filled with passion,
the pain began to dissipate,

and her heart began to feel light again.
Like, a rainbow in the sky after a storm.

At that very moment,
enlightenment fell upon her.

Her pain was part of her purpose,

and her past experiences had turned into her power.

This was what her soul had been craving.

* * *

She rose in the morning,
like a phoenix rising from the ashes,
reborn from the fires of her past.

Filled with a fierce fascination to live as her real authentic self,
living her purpose, pursuing her dreams, and knowing without a doubt,
that there was something magical hidden inside of her.

So, it began,
this intense, passionate courtship,
between herself and the paper.

Love was in the air,
desire filled her eyes, as she connected to her soul.
Devoted to making this love last forever,

she committed daily to this relationship.
Never, had she connected to anyone on such a profound level,
the depth of this bond was becoming immovable, nothing else mattered.

Her only focus was between herself and the pages,
her heart leaped with joy!
This bond was so strong, nothing could tear them apart,
she had met her soul mate.

# CHAPTER 6

## *Letting go, to gain*

*"With tears on these pages,
I sought out my inner wisdom.
Submerged in the depths of my very soul,
I found the universe within."
-Giovanna*

Even in black and white,
some people wouldn't get you.

It's taken me many years, and many difficult people, situations,
heartbreak, and setbacks,
for me to truly grasp patience.

The process, not the word.

First, the understanding, and then putting it into action.

There is power in learning patience.

You must choose to use it,
or choose to work for it.

Have patience with yourself,
have patience with your journey.

You will be tested repeatedly,
don't give up!

*The growth, is gained in the repetition,
have a renewed faith, that you are on the right path.*

What you are seeking,
you will surely find.
When you go within,
So, take your time.

*You are growing your spiritual muscles,
you are going through growing pains.
You are dropping your ego,
and gaining your spirit.*

With the growth of any muscle,
before you see growth,
you will feel pain.

Embrace that pain, as a sign of growth,
and challenge yourself to push harder.

Let go of your insecurities,
and let in self-love.

Let the gentle breeze
refresh your spirit

allow it to move you
in the right directions.

When you become comfortable,
being uncomfortable,
That is when the magic begins,
that is when you begin to witness
your own strength.

*When you learn the language of the universe,
you find where the keys to happiness are hidden.*

Finding it within, you move forward on your journey,
Continuing to unlock the codes and riddles of life.

What are you?
*Do you know?*

Better question, *who are you?*

>Who you are,
>is not who, you were.

>What they say to you,
>is not always the truth.

>Who you were,
>isn't, who you will become.

>Who you aren't,
>is no longer important.

>Who you become,
>is a sum of what you are.

>What you've lost,
>is no longer relevant.


>What you are
>can be only answered one way,

>by answering this question,
>*Who am I?*

>*Who determines, who you are?*
>YOU DO!

*Our stories are intertwined,*
*and woven together with each other souls.*
*So, healing yourself will have a ripple effect,*
*on healing the world.*

*Rise up to your ultimate potential*
*It's time!*


You are needed
You are supported

You are protected
You are congratulated

All those years of being misunderstood,
mistreated and manipulated.

Within those years I have learned,
that the judgment is on them.

That misunderstanding; is their own.
It has nothing to do with me.

I am now dancing in my greatness!
I'm not afraid to shine bright, and step into my purpose!


Because I no longer have to be someone I am not,
or no longer fearful of the opinions of others.

> If we love, and accept our self,
> for our differences, flaws, and insecurities,
> and we find empowerment in them,
> we run into growth literally!

We no longer care what others say;
they become muted by self-love.
> While on this journey, we are meeting the ego,
> shedding the traumas, pain, and misunderstanding.
> After, we are left with strength, and achievement,
> we are growing, feel empowered with every step you take.

*You are now learning with inner understanding, compassion,*
*and growth, the outer understanding*
*has the potential to be world changing!*

I know I do not fit in the "box" of social norms,
and I embrace that!

I scream that on the top of my lungs with pride and joy!
I am no longer, shameful of my differences.

I am no longer, making excuses for my power!
I must use them, now that I am following my purpose.

*I needed to stand out to been seen!*
*I needed to go through pain,*
*to be a witness of my own strength.*

*I needed to be stripped of everything,*
*to learn I am not attached to anything.*

**As things were taken away,**
**I gained more and more clarity.**

What I've learned on this journey of growth, and expansion,
is the hatred and misunderstanding wasn't directed towards me.
It is an outer reality, for the person who is judging me.

I am being used, as a reflection, a mirage, crossing one another's paths to be a blessing and/or a lesson for us both.

**A learning experience,**

It is both good, and bad, and both will aid in gaining wisdom,
with different directions leading you down different paths.

We all are someone else's blessing,
we are someone else's sign of hope.

You are the teacher,
and the student.

**A message to change, and become,**
**a glimpse of an angel here on earth.**

Whether, you see it at the time or not,
or whether you accept the mission.

*We are all parts to the puzzle,*
*and we all are here to love, teach and heal.*

But first,
we must heal ourselves.

*We are all going through a similar healing process,
at different stages, points and even lifetimes.*

*Connected to create a bigger picture,
and complete an even bigger puzzle!*

Notice the final product, and you will start
to make sense of all of the scattered pieces.

We are puzzles, within puzzles,
within puzzles.

We learn something new every day,
we meet someone new every day.

We will come across daily,
signs and gentle reminders.

Reminding us, that they are present,
and here to aid in our growth.
Walking us, along the path, toward meeting our highest self.

In our healing, and in our remembering,
there is refreshing and renewing of self.

The lessons that we go through,
are here to help us learn and remember.

They are guiding us,
so, we may help guide others.

Again,
interconnected.

*We are being taught patience, through our experiences,
our setbacks, our mistakes, our own flaws, and our free will.*

All of these,
eventually, determines our outcome.

But Spirit/God/Source/Universe/Angels
does not want us to fail.

They've already given us the victory,
and tools needed to succeed and prosper.

*We must remember!*
*They don't want us to lose faith and give up.*

**They are aware of our flaws,**
**and our human understanding.**

*They know the steps we must walk,*
*to gain the keys to personal freedom,*

**and they are walking daily with us.**

*The key to patience is understanding,*
*understanding,*
*that we know nothing.*

And from understanding,
gaining compassion,
for yourself and
eventually others.

**It's a process,**
**that sometime takes a lifetime to realize.**

*It's gained, lost,*
*and then found again.*

This enlightenment,
and new found understanding,
can't be contained it's contagious,
and it needs to be spread.

If we turn on our student hats,
instead, of acting like reckless teenagers,
we can slow down,
and read the signs.
Heeding the warnings
and follow our intuition.

To grow our resilience, and our character,
we are tested and retested again and again.
To see if we changed, defaulted,
upgraded, or reprogrammed, our mentality.

*Look even deeper,*
*and you will start to see,*
*the synchronicities,*
*between you and me.*

Do you see the connections, and lessons in the reality around you?

If you silence your mind,
you'll feel them right beside you.

Guidance, reassurance,
infinite love shining through.

Their cheering you on!
You will always be protected!

*I appreciate my life and all the hardships Spirit has brought me through.*
*I love my life, and everyone spirit has brought in to it.*
*No matter if it was briefly or lengthy,*
*Good or bad*

**The connections or disconnect taught me,**
**more than anyone could have told me.**
My growth has been massive,
I found my voice,
My strength,
My beauty,
My soul,
and my purpose.

*Becoming inspired is a process,*
*Becoming enlightened is a journey,*
*Becoming your true self is priceless.*

We are truly blessed,
when we come across someone who touches not only our heart,
but our soul.

Someone who not only tells us,
but demonstrates the true beauty of kindness.

Showing us healing,
through compassion,
and sharing empowerment
through understanding.
Instantly, becoming the catalyst,
for your personal and spiritual growth.

*Notebook Time:*

*Have you met someone like I've described?*
*Someone who instantly spoke to your soul?*
*Where you could tell it was a Divine connection*

*Write it down in your notebook,*

*The name of that soul and situation that took place.*
*Start to see the connections, and you will begin to notice that everything, really does happen for a reason, and it's usually in your favour if not, your protection.*

*Souls cross our path for many reasons, messages, reminders, affirmations, guidance,*
*healing, compassion, love, understanding, and to push us in the right direction.*

*Become grateful for the connections, and create your*
*own connection,*
*through listening to your intuition.*
*Listen to the whispers, if you feel an urge to call or write someone, do it.*


*If you see someone*
*and have the urge to say something nice,*
*don't think twice!*

*Go over and make someone smile,*
*you never know you may have just saved someone's life.*

# CHAPTER 7

## It's time, there's a shift

> *"Let go of it all,*
> *for your own personal freedom and for your own sanity."*
> *-Giovanna*

It's time,
there's a shift.

I feel it,
can you?

Like the strong winds, right before a storm,
and changing of the seasons throughout the year,

Death, and birth,
Life and lessons in all.

*It's time*
*we started*
*to get less distracted*
*and more focused.*

*It's time to do less blaming,*
*and more forgiving of yourself.*

*It's time to let go of the pain,*
*and make room for healing.*

*It's time to let go of the heartache,*
*and start learning to love yourself again.*

*It's time,*
*to let go of the past.*
*Let go of it all,*
*for your own personal freedom and sanity.*

You do not have to justify your pain,
You do not have to justify your anger.

But you can only be the sum,
Of all that you give out into the world.

If that is all, you give out,
what do you think you will get in return?

*You will find your self
confused and miserable.*

You will always be in pain,
if that is all you focus on.

## *Seek and speak*

---

*You don't have to continue the years of pain,
after the battle is over.*

*You don't have to keep fighting a war,
that was meant never to be fought.*

---

Put down the sword,
put down the knife.

It is ok, you are safe,
you are protected.

Once we allow ourselves, to let go of all the past emotions, we can allow ourselves to release, the baggage we've been carrying for so long.

*This next destination you are headed to,
requires no baggage, just bring yourself!*

*Gratitude*

*I am so grateful I woke up today with purpose
I am so grateful for today!
I am so grateful I have the drive the meet my destiny, and the push to
bring out my passions.
I am grateful for the strength I gained, and the success that I have.
I am grateful for the motivation, and the opportunity to make it happen.
I am grateful for my body.*

# CHAPTER 8

## The antidote for our INTERNAL pain

*"I revived my vulnerability,
and found an antidote for self-love!
It's now time to share with you my remedies."*
-Giovanna

This is a special report,

A sign from above,
we've found the antidote,
It is you!
Now take a sip,
it's time to heal.

Like I said in the intro,
this book is meant to bring you;
**personal freedom, empowerment, healing** and begin
the process to awaken and **liberate your soul.**

It was written,
because there is a dire need
for **healing in the world** today,
and it **starts with our self.**

So **here is your wake-up call,**
Angel signs, 11:11
**intuitive feelings,**
call it what you want, put a label and categorize it.

*You have got to remember we are all connected*

This is for the collective Human Race,
and generations to come.
Spoken by the voice within.
However, you receive this,

> however, you hear the voice,
> and see the universe,
> silence your mind it's time to listen.

*This is a message,*
*written to be received by your soul.*

This will only be taken as false evidence,
If you are unable to face your own T.R.U.T.H.S.
and deny the connection.

*I cut out my own toxic pain,*
*the very demons that were killing me inside,*
*my repressed, not so hidden insecurities,*
*and I dissected them.......*
*In hopes of finding a cure,*
*and saving someone's life.*

> "I revived my vulnerability,
> and found an antidote for self-love!
> It's now time to share with you my remedies."

**"When self-hate is multiplied, and self-love,**
**is no longer added into the equation**
**DIS-EASE will always be the end result!"**

Here is the proof;
because some people don't want to believe it,
until, it happens to them.
*So, let's see if this has happened to you?*

**This is a Pop Quiz,**
**school is now in session.**
**Time to pay attention,**
**this is not in the curriculum,**
**So, take notes.**

With the mass majority's drawn to quick fixes and modern medicine,
*we forget to look for the problem.*

> *When you dig to find the problem,*
> *you're one step closer to the solution.*

---

*True healing, is about addressing the core issue.*

For a lot of us, we don't even know where to begin,
and that's ok, neither did I.
But the whole *"If I don't talk about it, it doesn't exist, or it's not my problem"*
is childish.

### This affects us all.

Think of this as your first Doctor's appointment towards a healthier life!
I tricked you,
You needed a check-up, and I knew you wouldn't come.

### It's time to get a game plan together.

Your notebook will help you find your own cures to the diseases
you  have. It will aid in getting you started towards writing your own T.R.U.T.H.S, and
provide you a blank page to write the next chapter
of your life.

**No more excuses!!**

It is time to create the health you want to see,
not the health controlled by your T.R.U.T.H.S.

**You possess the Keys to YOUR SELF HEALING!**

Affirmation:

I am powerful
I am in charge of my own life
I am the co-creator of my reality
I release old mentalities
I release hatred and regret
I release anything holding me back
I release any relationships that are no longer for my growth and ascension
I make room for abundance
And remain humble and grateful for all that I do have.

# CHAPTER 9

## T·R·U·T·H·S OR DARE

**T.R.U.T.H.S.**
**TRIALS REVEALING UNDERSTANDING THROUGH HEALING SELF**

*"Allow yourself to become vulnerable, don't hold back,*
*it's time to start to heal our souls."*
*-Giovanna*

We are all here for two reasons;
healing and understanding.

Let's face the facts,
and put a name to the face of the beast within.

I believe we can shorten and/or extend our lifespan,
all through our thinking.
Again, just my thoughts,
I am not a doctor.

But I do know,
I was killing myself with my negative, unhealthy self-talk.

I was sitting in the darkness alone, suffocated by my own silence,
with no one to talk to, lost and ready to give up.

Do you ever feel abandoned? Have you or are you being abused or mistreated?
Do you give all of yourself to others and receive nothing in return?

    Are you dissatisfied with your life?

    Are you struggling with self-hate?

    Were you ever taught self-love?


As a side effect to the unaddressed trials that we go through, it can
manifest into; acid reflux, migraines, anxiety, depression, fear, chronic pain, disease, disorders, cancer, or worse a heart attack.

There are so many things that can make us feel isolated,

forgotten, unloved, unworthy, less than,
tormented, and bullied.
There are so many situations and
T.R.U.T.H.S that I have not gone through.

Maybe, by hearing some of my T.R.U.T.H.S,
it will inspire you, to start to connect the dots
to your own traumas, disorders, and illnesses.

Pin pointing the source, of what has caused you pain,
suffering, disorders, disease, cancer, and feelings of worthlessness
for so many years.

*With a new realization, and outlook we can start to change our diagnosis.*

---

*"With knowledge comes responsibility,
with understanding comes healing."*

---

*I feel the pain of the world, and
I see the programmed destination,
and I want to change it!
I want you to change it!
Let's change the destination in the GPS.
Let's master reset,
time to clean our internal hard drive.
All ages are invited!*

I dare you;

Let's get **R.I.P.E** with YOUR SOUL.

Raw, Intimate, Painful and Enjoy

Let's really **M.E.E.T** YOUR SOUL,

Magnify Enlighten Examine and Trust

*"Facing my T.RU.T.H.S. has been one of the hardest things in my life,
it has also been the most liberating!"*

Let's uncover who YOU really are,
not, who others want YOU to be!

*Let's dissect, why you feel the way you do,*
*about yourselves today.*

*What is the correlation,*
*between your mental, physical and spiritual health?*

*What is the connection*
*or disconnection between your happiness?*

Let's take a journey to the core issues,
face our past and conquer our inner demons.

Let's take their power away and challenge their very existence!

**It's time to RECLAIM your power!**

Let's unlock the mental chains that have been holding you back,
and re-learn YOU possess the keys!
*You just have to remember where you put them.*

**This is about understanding yourself,**
**YOUR own health;**
**Mentally, physically, spiritually.**

*Let's see how they all work together,*
*How, it is all connected.*

What do you pick?
TRUTH OR DARE

BOTH? I dare you to write your T.R.U.T.H.S


*Notebook Time;*

*Begin to write out some of your trials,*
*What do you keep hidden? What do you ignore? What do you not talk*
*about?*
*What have you lived through and survived?*
*Write it down*

# CHAPTER 10

## *Befriending the beast*

> *"I fought the battle, and made it out alive."*
> *-Giovanna*

Tales of a Spoonie warrior,
Writings about my autoimmune, Lupus battle.

No one will do it for you, either you cover up the problem,
or deal with it and heal yourself.
Again, another choice,
we all have free will.

> Do we face our problems?
> Or do we hide them and complain?

*I've done both,*

> with willpower and the amazing earth,
> we can all be healthy.

*I embrace myself, just as I am,*
*even in the uncertainty.*

> My invisible illness is not who I am,
> It's just part of my story, a path towards my greatness.

*Through my pain,*
*I found my purpose.*
*One day at a time.*

Back in 2015
I've learned the hard way, time and time again;
That some days I just need to accept that I cannot do it. Both physically, or mentally. I've learned the hard way, that I need to listen to my body. I am in tune with what I need and I am most certainly aware of what my body does not want. I've learned to be grateful and appreciate the days I feel normal, and I celebrate the good days; the days I am not in pain. The days I am not flaring, the days I am still alive.

> *Our struggle is where our strength comes from,*
> *embrace it.*

Here we go,
I'm learning to let go,
show my T.R.U.T.H.S,
Speak my truths,
and live my truths.

*My health battle has affected my joints, ligaments, bones, stomach, and mind the pain ran deep.*

Truth is I am pretty normal,
I have the same insecurities as everyone else.
I have allowed my lack of self-love and self-respect to get the best of me.

I have created, and allowed disease to grow within,
and it has come to the surface.

**No more hiding or pretending that my illness does not exist, or that it doesn't affect me.**

*I take full responsibility!*

*All of this was necessary,
the disease that manifested,
the pain I battled.
I needed to go through this journey,
to find how deep my strength ran.*

I've battled through years of this constant invisible chronic pain, pain so
Bad there wasn't a part of me that didn't hurt, my hands, my toes, my
ligaments, every single bone in my body I felt an undesirable pain. My
joints swelled, and I was unable to lift anything for weeks and
even months at a time. I had flu like symptoms, no appetite for weeks, body aches, chills, no strength to even lift a cup of water. My body
was here, but my mind drifted to other places, I was living in hell. Weeks went by and soon turned into months, months turned into years. Being
pain-free, was now only a distant memory. Crying was my only way of letting the pain go, no medicine would take it away.

**I see now all I gained, as I lay there thinking I was losing myself.**

From this journey, I have a deep understanding and greater compassion.
Being unable to work, or do pretty much anything, I learned new hobbies, I
started meditation, learned about the benefits of crystal healing, read up on
healing through food. As much as I wanted to write or do yoga as suggested I was unable, not enough strength in my hands for that yet.

I was literally broken, falling apart,
when I made the connection that I was being taught patience,
hours, and hours and hours to myself, I started to find myself.

I had said no to medicine during the first year, after being prescribed way
too many medications with too many side effects.
I saw firsthand how Dr's, had no idea what was wrong with me, and they
only wanted to cover it up and make money.
So, I read and learned about the disease controlling my body and myself.

*It was at my lowest that I heard the whispers of guidance.*

---

## YOU HAVE THE POWER TO HEAL YOUR SELF.

---

We have everything we need,
the medicine comes from the earth.

*I had to go to the source of the disease;*
*My body, My mind, and My soul.*

My autoimmune disease is literally textbook description of my mental state,
my body was fighting against itself.
For years, I've been in this inner battle with myself,
and eventually, it showed its ugly face as LUPUS.

*Most hide their insecurities, and I still do at times.*
*But I wanted to be transparent,*
*I wanted to empower others, and show them*
*that no one is perfect.*

We all have flaws, but when we share them, it highlights our strength.

I realized,

**My power is in my T.R.U.T.H.S. and my strength is in my healing.**

That is why I share them, in hopes to empower others,
to show and share their truths and no longer be the silent victim.

*The biggest step forward, is taking responsibility for our diseases, admitting we did not know, and learn to heal, rather than cover up.*

Most of the time, the truth is not pretty,
But it is the truth,
and that is real.

One of my superpowers
I've mastered,
is power of the mind.
The universe has taught me this,
while overcoming my autoimmune disease.
Most days I am in pain,
but I don't take meds.

## Mind over matter

Other days,
I allow meds to help me cope with the pain.
It's such a weird pain,
I feel it in my bones,
my joints, ligaments, and
my nerves.

I feel it where no one can see,
*Yes, a reflection of my buried truths* I am working to uncover.

I don't like to talk about my illness,
I don't even like to admit, when I have a bad day.
I feel it makes me weak,
but I've realized I'm not helping myself.
I am sick,
even though I may not look it,
I am not ok.
But I'm not giving up,
my pain medication is my mind.

*Mind over matter, right?*

I tell myself this is not me; I am stronger than this disease,
I can do this…. And then my head hits the bed for a 20-minute nap with
Alarm set, and I wake up the next day 13 hours later never hearing my
multiple alarms feeling like I only slept for 30 minutes.
SELF TALK

I am not ok,
but I am ok,

I will be ok,
I am not giving up.

Healing is on its way,
I am stronger than this,
I am a warrior,
I am the hero in the story.

I am healing with every meal I eat,
and I am alive to talk about it.
I am blessed,
I love my body.

This disease broke me for over a year straight,
it had me on my on my knees praying just to be done,
and then years later, I'm coming back,
by the grace of God.

With a new outlook, totally different foods that I put into my body, and new books to feed my mind. My body has taught me a lot, and it got my attention. I'm on my own journey, but from it, I'm reminded daily, when I cheat with certain foods, the sudden effect those allergies do to my body. I am the one who will pay, I'm the one that will flare, I will feel the pain, it can't be covered up, I'm the one who will set myself back.

This pain has reminded me, how truly powerful I am,
and when I finally master it and no longer fight against it,
working with it consistently,
I'll level up!

Thank you, God, for your healing,
compassion, and encouragement.

These things we carry today,
one day, we won't have to carry,
and we will just have the muscles,
a byproduct of the pain we endured for so long.

*I'm in the spiritual gym sweating my butt off,*
*but with hard work and dedication,*
*I know I am a beast in the making!*
*My body just needs to align with my mind.*

Everyone has their own battles,
their own enemy,
their own scars.

My enemy
is myself,
and my body is at war with itself.

An endless battle,
of aches, pain,
and depression.

I am torn,
I am beaten,
I am broken,

But,
I am
not dead.

Every morning,
I am blessed with new day,
and I choose to see it as a present.

*Consciously, choosing to see my life how I wanted to see it,*
*rather than the reality I was living in,*
*was a big step.*

*But it was also liberating!*

---

*I am far from mighty,*
*but I have the drive and will of 1000 buffalo.*

---

I grew from my ashes,
and I want to empower others,
to do the same.

There is no shame in being raw, and authentic,
it should be celebrated!
With more vulnerability,
there can be more internal healing for all!

*My wisdom is ever growing*
*My pain is slowly healing*
*My truths are being spoken.*

**Note to self on a bad day**

You are alive for a reason
You are a whole being
You a soul within a physical body
You are not your illness
You are not your disease
You are not your setback,
You are MORE, so much more.
You are abundant
You are healing
You are learning to love parts of yourself, you have been at war with
You are allowing the parts of you that no longer suit your growth, to drift away
You are amazing
You are perfect
And don't ever forget that

**Allow yourself the compassion, understanding, and forgiveness, to heal**

>Sending you love and healing energy
>Xoxo Giovanna

# CHAPTER 11

## *Trusting the process*

"You are a ray of hope in someone's life never forget that.
Their darkness needs your light."
-Giovanna

A message, to all the caterpillars and butterflies in the world,

Please remember it is a process,
we all go through stages,
the cocoon stage is dark and scary,
and when you transform breaking free can be shocking.
When you get your wings use them.
We are all different, all amazingly unique,
some are more colorful than others, but none greater than the rest.
We have beauty in us all,
and every stage is necessary, and needed for our growth, and development.
Be at peace and learn to trust your wings.
I love you.

Sometimes, the greatest step is admitting, that<br>
**We are lost**<br>
**We are broken and**<br>
**We are scared.**

We are also amazing beings, each and everyone,
no matter our faults or past.

We must admit our fears,<br>
so they lose power over<br>
our lives.

I am walking this path,
I am speaking my truths,
I am taking my pain, and creating a masterpiece,
one piece at a time.

Trust and believe,<br>
no matter what religion,<br>
no matter what age, or race,<br>
if your path is difficult

you have a higher calling,
and greatness within you.
From this difficulty;
you will master patience,
share love, practice compassion,
learn self-healing, find acceptance,
give forgiveness, and practice self-respect.

Everyone, is different with unique stories and pain,
find peace in knowing,
there is a reason for it all.

*"When we acknowledge our weaknesses,
it pushes us towards our healing"
-Giovanna*

We need to remind ourselves,
Of all the transformations, we've already gone through and survived.
We need to remind ourselves how much beauty is in the process,
and at any stage, that we are growing, this is all part of the process.

As I release,
I create a clear path for who I will become,
letting go of all that was,
to let in all that is.
I am FREE

**Let the breakdowns happen,
break out and break free from the mental chains!
There is great healing in freedom.**

*You've got to start somewhere,
you've got to recognize a problem
before finding a solution*

---

*If you speak your truths,
no one can use it to overpower you.*

---

*Your weakness becomes
your greatest power.*

**We break, to become whole once more.**

*I support my growth,*
*I release my fear,*
*I celebrate my death,*
*I embody spirit,*
*I allow my higher self,*
*to guide me.*

We all have our battles,
Some are physical some are mental
One thing is for certain;
We are all human,
and deep down inside
there is beautiful soul.

**Dig, break, and remove,**
**until you find your self-love.**

*Do you hear the soft, gentle whisper?*
*Let go....*
*You are protected and guided*
*All is well.*

*Notebook Time:*

Tear out 2 pieces of paper from your notebook

On the first piece of paper

make a list of all of your fears in detail
what are you scared of? What is holding back from your own happiness?

On the second piece of paper

make a list of your strengths (10 or more)
What makes you special? What are your unique talents?

*Take the first paper with your fears written out,
and rip it up and throw it away.*

*Now, grab your second piece of paper with your strengths
and read that list out loud in front of the mirror.*

*You are now only left with all your strengths*

*keep this close and anytime you are feeling insecure,
pull this out and remember how once wrote down your strengths,
you were able to throw out your fears!
Literally!*

# CHAPTER 12

## *Who are you?*

*"Distorted realities and fake illusions of how we see ourselves,
ill affect how we are seen by others"*
*-Giovanna*

When you learn to listen to your inner voice, connection happens.

It's that little voice inside of you,
tune in.

When you learn you have a voice, healing occurs.

When, you use your voice,
change happens.

your soul is calling you,
your initiation is aligned,
now all you have to do, is trust.


I know this is crazy right

am I Fake.... nope
am I Authentic....yes
am I Different.....very

You can call it how you see it,
your eyes tell lies,

**You will find the truth,
in your distorted vision of me.
For I am a reflection of how you see yourself.**

What you hate about me,
you hate within yourself.

*We are mirrors, teachers, and lessons all wrapped into one.*

Learn to love yourself once more!
Find your light,
and see the love in all.
Go within your darkness,
your soul is waiting.

*Raw and unfiltered*
*It's not that I'm perfect,*
*I'm flawed in all the right ways.*

From each lesson in life that we go through,
we get a parting gift, a prize for making it through the process, such as
patience, love, perseverance, determination, strength, resilience, a lesson etc.

**What was sent to break me,**
**Strengthened me.**

**What was meant to kill me,**
**Empowered me.**

We all have the gifts and tools to get to the next level

*Do you use them?*
*Use them!*

When met with anger,
find peace.
When met with hate,
find understanding.
When met with struggle,
find resilience.

Change your reaction
Change your outcome
You have, all you need within you.

You are enough,

TODAY, YESTERDAY AND
TOMORROW.
Believe it.

---

*It wasn't that I didn't know who I was,*
*I was surrounded by people who didn't want to see the authentic me.*

---

So, I felt lost, not realizing,
the wrong people had surrounded me.
I was not in the right environment to grow.

*If people only see you one way,*
*change it and change your reality.*

I'm misunderstood, I'm taken for granted, I'm hated
and was once made fun of.
But opinions, and judgments, are part of the process, part of the work,
part of the healing.
I am far from perception, and I am bigger than reality.
I have my good days, and my bad days,
I am partly still human.
But I am facing my T.R.U.T.H.S and,
I am walking into my light.

**One soul at a time I will hold space for you**
**I love you**
**I appreciate**
**I see you**

*Notebook Time:*

*Rewrite the script, time to change up the characters in your story*

*1. What are some of the lies people have said about you?*
*What lies have you been believing? When were you told these lies?*

*Now,*
*2. Write down how you want to be seen*
*examples; strong, confident, smart, funny, educated, good looking, athletic,*
*etc.*

*Make a list and create your new reality*

*We tend to have our faults on repeat,*
*it's time to change the music in your head,*
*by claiming your best qualities,*
*and letting go of the lies you were taught to hold on to.*

# CHAPTER 13

## *You must break, in order to heal*

*"I only speak my truths,
I'm learning that I can dance in my darkness,
and heal my own soul.
But only after,
I swallowed my truths and nearly poisoned myself!"
-Giovanna*

When was the last time you danced with yourself?

Have you ever fallen in love with your own soul?

**We have to learn to dance in our own darkness and become our own light.**

---

We must learn to self-love instead, of self-hate,
and as we forgive, we learn to let go.

---

We have to call bs on our own actions,
reactions, and the things we were taught!

We must face our own T.R.U.T.H.S.,
hold up mirror, and look at our own reflection,
to find healing, peace, and self-love.

Question the very existence of your thoughts,
and why you treat yourself, the way that you do.

Listen to your inner voice, replay your self-talk, and
begin to hold yourself accountable.

Face your inner demons,
wrestle with your self-hate,
and become vulnerable.

*Sometimes, the only way around it,
is through it,
and the only way to overcome it,
is to defeat it.*

*Right now, it's not about finding that peace,
it's about finding that anger, that rage, that pain,
that regret.
That deep feeling, you've been suppressing,
dissect that very emotion.*

*Break, that emotion down.
Find the source and seek out the truth.*

*We are all able to heal ourselves,
our souls know exactly what we need.*

*We must silence our minds,
and listen with our hearts*

*Sometimes the greatest step is admitting,
that we are lost,
we are broken and
we are scared.*

At the same time, we must also remind ourselves,
that we are amazing beings,
each, and every one of us,
no matter our faults, setbacks, past,
where you came from or who your parents are.

---

*We must admit our fears, so they lose power over our lives.*

---

*I am walking this path,
I am speaking my truths,
I am taking my pain, and creating a masterpiece, one piece at a time.*

**This pain you're feeling,
don't hide it, don't suppress it,
Feel it! Listen to it!**

*What is it trying to tell you?*

In feeling your emotions,
do you also feel your power!?

You have the power over these emotions, and feelings.
You control your mind,
not, the other way around.

*Gain control and let go.*
*Let go of how,*
*let go of when,*
*let go of what ifs.*
*What if it will happen?*
*What if it is already in the making?*

You are already healing,
you are growing your self-love,
you are finding
your own happiness.

***All of this and more!***
***On the other side, of that very emotion you are suppressing.***

Find it and dig that diamond out!
You are the buried treasure!

No one, will do it for you,
Either, YOU decide to cover up the problem,
or deal with it and heal yourself.

*Again, another choice,*
*we have free will.*

Do we face our problems?

Or hide them and complain?

I've done both
with willpower and mother Gaia (mother earth goddess)
We can all be healthy.

*You are one step away from a breakthrough,*
*You are one inch away from the end,*
*Don't give up.*

Keep going,
Keep fighting.

*Do you see it?*
*Can you feel it?*

Dig deep,
find that reserved energy,
that final push needed,
to boost you, into the next chapter,
into the next dimension.
The catalyst for your growth
has always been you.

*Pull back, and push forward,*
*If your breaking ....*

Allow it,
it is time.

We are all going through transformations,
breaking, crying, shedding, healing, and growing!
Trust the process.

Notebook Time:

It is time to break, write whatever comes to mind.
Let the words flow as your pen hits the paper

What are you feeling? Where do you feel pain? Who caused you pain?

We tend to keep things bottled up and tucked away,
now is the time to put it on paper.

Write a letter to the person that has been causing you pain,
write down all that you want to say, even if you never send it,
you have released it from your body,
you are one step closer towards your own personal liberation.

How can you heal a pain
that you don't know the source?
You can't, you will only cover it up.

# CHAPTER 14

## *Your pain has a purpose*

> *"And with that flame,*
> *she lit up the world around her,*
> *she was a beacon of hope,*
> *a teller of truths"*
> *-Giovanna*

It is ok to be mad at the way you were treated!
To be angry at the way someone disrespected you,
or even how you've disrespected yourself.

**Feel those feelings and release the pain that was attached to them.**
**Say it with me,**
**I am not those feelings.**

**It's a ball and chain, and you possess the key,**
**FREE YOURSELF.**

*You're not alone,*
*everyone has their darkness,*
*some have learned to dance in it,*
*others are stuck in it.*

Those who do not face their own darkness,
will try and throw it on you.
Remember,
You do not have to accept it.

*I've transformed my experiences into art,*
*my pain turned into words,*
*my diversity into wisdom.*

Until, I transformed my pain,
I was in pain and lost.

I gained control when I used my pain,
rather than being used by my pain.

I am powerful,
instead of powerless.

Is not all light work,
It's heavy, it's dark, its ugly
but it is,
healing.

*It is healing, all of the parts of you that for years you repressed and dismissed.*

**On the other side of your fears,
are your deepest desires.**

**On the other side of your self-hate,
is really self-love.**

*Take the leap of faith,
   lose the fear, and doubt.*

---

*Dance with your own success,
celebrate your own victories,
and step into your purpose.*

---

*Declare out loud,*

I AM possible
I can easily do this,
I've got this!
I am successful, in all I set my mind to.


*How can we teach, show, live, and heal?
If we have not experienced that very human pain, emotion and/or struggle?*
Depression, guilt, fear.
All emotions and can be life altering.

I've felt them, I've struggled with self-love and self-hate,
I can relate, to a part of that darkness.

Some may say I am different,
because I am vulnerable.
I say
I am light in a world full of darkness.
I make mistakes
I am not perfect.
I share my truths to empower,
I am healing, through living as my authentic life,
and through my daily actions, allowing others to see
my light,
because actions always speak louder than words.

**When, I allowed the universe to move through me,
when I permitted myself to let go,
to be happy, and speak my truths
My world suddenly expanded.**

Don't be afraid to release, forgive, and let go of your burdens, or guilt.

*If you cannot seem to let them go, ask yourself
is it even yours to be carrying?*

By allowing yourself, to slowly let go of the years of doubt and guilt,
you are also allowing, the healing to begin.
It is a process, take your time, and have patience with yourself,
you are releasing years of emotions.

*Affirmations:*

*I allow myself the compassion to grow
I allow myself to befriend my darkness
I allow myself freedom from the chains of my tongue
I allow myself to go through the phases and heal
I allow myself to let go of human understanding.*

# CHAPTER 15

## *Building up self*

*"Already defeating the war mentally,
you just have to fight the battle within."
-Giovanna*

*You will be recreating your own blueprint,
examining the foundation of your relationship with self,
and examining the very bricks you've been using to build your "House."*

How many people have been there?
Honestly?? No one else is listening, and I'm only in your head lol

How many people live with an invisible illness? *-I do*

*Something that mentally now gives them DISEASE?
Migraines, chronic pain, mental disease, even cancer,
These are deadly battles within our bodies, within our minds.*

Begin to Face your trials,
and come face to face with your T.R.U.T.H.S.

*Medicine will take care of the symptoms,
but this book is about going deeper.
To the internal cause and becoming aware of your internal battles.
It is about seeing how you project them into your own life.
By relearning,
you can change,
the outcomes,
of the wars, you are battling internally.*

That's right, if we want to change the outcome,
we have to learn to fight in the war.

*But I will help in your preparation, one stepping stone at a time.*

Through my experience and my battles,
I will share with you my pain, and purpose.

> Maybe this will encourage you,
> to find your own line of defense against
> your own T.R.U.T.H.S.
> Revealing your ultimate power
> So, you will be able to go into every battle
> Ready, willing and able.

I know, I am not alone, and I definitely know, that there are so many souls that are fighting their own battle alone, and many that have lost the war and are now home.

Share your stories; I want to hear your T.R.U.T.H.S.

There is valid emotion in each pain you feel and
secrets are revealed, with each truth you uncover.
Every sleepless night, every fallen tear,
is a part of your story.

> Like any math problem,
> figure out the equation
> and punch in your numbers.

> *Affirmations:*
>
> *I am learning*
> *I am understanding*
> *I am growing*
> *I am forgiving myself and others*
> *I am healing*
> *I am allowing healing to happen*
> *I am letting go*
> *I affirm my healing*
> *I affirm my power*
> *I affirm my personal freedom*
> *I am facing my truths head on.*

# CHAPTER 16

*I am*

> "My T.R.U.T.H.S. lived out to be a reality
> almost to the T."
> -Giovanna

I am my greatest enemy,

What about you?
Be honest,

*You've started to write out your truths,*
*now look them all up.*

T.R.U.T.H.S
Trials reveal understanding
Through healing self

**Mentally dissect and see how the answers,**
**are hidden within the problem,**
**Within your (T.R.U.T.H.S)**

We need to face the pain of those who have broken us.
Whether it has been physical, sexual, verbal, or mental,
whoever has broken your self-esteem, whoever took away your light,
whoever you have lost or who has left you.
We need to go deep into your minds,
and pull out that very real T.R.U.T.H.
and deactivate the ticking time bomb.

*I've been battling myself, and my Truths,*
*For more than half of my life, majority of the time, in silence.*

I have managed, to lose my power, rediscover and then become fearful of the power I possess!
It's been a struggle, and a real mental battle.
Some days, I've wanted to give up.
But I'm coming back, hotter than ever,
You can't put this fire out!
I've learned, I can be in control, not the other way around.
I create my own reality!

*It has taken me many years, to believe this statement,
and even longer, to apply it, and say it out loud.*

You can too!
No matter what age,
no matter what belief,
no one is left out,
everyone is able,
to receive this internal healing,
and much needed download.

*I still have to remind myself daily
How amazing I am. It's easy to fall back into old habits.
To use negative thoughts and self-talk to keep me from my own self-happiness*

I survived this far,
I have walked toward my healing
By walking within

Yes, some weeks/months or even years, it felt as if I was crawling,
But it started with effort.

I was once stuck in my own darkness,
killing myself from the inside out.
But now, I am overcoming and healing my body of Lupus, an invisible autoimmune disease,
that for years had been attacking my entire body and nervous system

My TRUTHS, lived out to be a reality
almost to the T.


*Words have power!!!
Repeat after me!*

**My words, hold great power,
I can speak things into existence,
and change my reality.**

*Please listen when I say this.*

*It's time to take responsibility,
for what you have already spoken into your reality.*

*Let this sink into to your subconscious,
Let it soak into the soil of your soul.*

*Watch what you give life to.*

*Be aware of the words that you speak.*

**We must nurture ourselves,**

**We must take care of our inner garden.**

**We must become our own organic soul food.**

*I found myself,*
*while sifting through all of my fragmented pieces,*
*of what I thought was myself but labeled as trash.*

At my lowest breaking point; dis-eased and alone,
I found my greatest clarity.

I was depressed, in constant excruciating chronic pain,
and I was told things wouldn't change;
this was my life, take the meds and accept it and get used to it.
For years, they were unable to diagnose me, feeding me pain pills to cover it up.
I was supposed to learn to adapt, accept, and essentially move on.

Take all these medicines, with all these side effects, and oh yes,
what you have is incurable.
Deal with it.

*All I wanted to do was escape!*
*And I couldn't ....*
*I was literally trapped.*

Hours turned into days,
days turned into weeks,
week turned into months,
and still no improvement.

---

*Silence crept up and*
*I was gently reminded to revisit all of my repressed memories.*

---

*Try it one more time,*
*go within, they whispered,*
*go within,*
*The healing you need is within.*

I started my painful journey,
into the deep dark unknown,
everyone that had broken me,
everyone that had taken my power,
Everyone who violated me,
anyone that had held me back, including myself,

*I was going to take it back!*

*Reclaim my power!*

*Relight my flame within.*

*I had to start with an internal flush.*
*I had to clear out all of the impurities that*
*I had ingested throughout my years.*
*It was time to heal my gut of all of my past*
*internal suffering,*
*all of my resentment, hostility, unresolved issues,*
*pain, anger, self-hate, and TRUTHS.*

*They needed to be faced*
*Head on.*
*(where I got the title to my book)*

*A Truth laxative, to flush it all out.*

*I fasted;*
*I fasted from food,*
*I fasted from music,*
*I fasted from social media*
*I fasted from TV,*
*I fasted from people.*

I NEEDED to regain my power,
I NEEDED to find my clarity,
I NEEDED to reignite my light again.

My strength would come, the answers, would be shown.

*It was time to meet up with my healing, during my walk within.*

As I allowed myself to revisit each one of my broken memories,
I honored the pain that came with them.
I reflected on the story that went with it,

> *I viewed it from an outside source.*
> *As a teacher, rather than the student,*
> *and I began to see the eagle eye's view.*
> *The connection between the struggle,*
> *and the strength that I have now.*

I permitted myself to feel the pain,
the very thing I had been running from and battling for so long.

> **I had to face it and allow myself to release and let go.**
>
> **Only I could give myself, the freedom I desired.**

I let go of the broken relationships,
unresolved issues, internal pain,
resentment, self-hate, mistakes,
any ties that held me back, and all feelings of obligation
**I chose to finally release them.**

> **They were sent to the trash bin, and permanently deleted.**

*Everything that I was clinging to both physically, and subconsciously,*
*ANYTHING I was still attached to I had to let it go.*

---

*It was time to clean out my spiritual closet,*
*and make room for my new wardrobe!"*

---

> Think about this......

If we outgrow old styles....
    *Why can't we outgrow ourselves?*

We grow out of our clothes, don't we?!
    *Why can't we outgrow people?*

We let go of broken items...
    *Why can't we let go of old broken habits that no   longer suit us?*

*Change up your closet,*
*get rid of anything you don't wear anymore,*
*anything that is torn, damaged,*
*out of date, or no longer fits.*
*Let it go*
*and make room*
*It's time for an upgrade!*

My daily affirmations

I affirm my healing
I affirm my growth
I affirm my power
I am a healer
I am healing
I am healed

I'm 30 and just now accepting, understanding and realizing,
It's ok for everyone not to like me,
and for others not to understand me.
It's ok to NOT BE FOR EVERYONE

**IF ONLY I had learned this sooner.**
It would have saved me years of unhappiness and self-hate.
But I've learned as I live and grow, to embrace, and love, who I am,
and who I am becoming.
I am me,
I am different, and I make no more excuses for my awesomeness.

# CHAPTER 17

## *You are what you eat*

>"The wisdom is found with-in the chaos"
>-Giovanna

I slowly began to reclaim my power,
as I let go of my ego.
*Which is not an easy task at all, let me tell you.*

---

*It's funny, how Spirit will make you sit and learn,*
*Spirit will free up your schedule and grab your attention!*
*When you ask for an upgrade, prepare to get a lesson and be tested.*

---

I've learned to find strength, in my T.R.U.T.H.S. (trials)
and in the process, the pieces began to come together,
I was starting to see the bigger picture.

I sorted through the disarray,
one by one, acknowledging the purpose.
Each one of my truth's, a piece to my puzzle,
I needed each piece, to complete the puzzle fully,
or else I would be missing a piece.
*It was all starting to make sense!*

It was only after I poured all the pieces out, that I saw the connection,
and knew I would be able to conquer the completion of this GIANT
life size puzzle. Connecting the dots, I started separating all the pieces,
and by using my intuition it all began to fit together, perfectly.
*My internal wars were being acted out,*
*and my body took center stage, as the battlefield.*

We have the power to create disease with ourselves,
and so, do the foods, that we put into our body.

*But just as easily,*
*we can create peace within ourselves,*
*and find healing and cures.*
*Each and every one;*
*We have the power,*
*We just have to reclaim it,*
*relearn and remember.*

When I chose to feed myself self-love, instead of self-hate,
my whole identity changed.
I acted differently,
I thought differently,
I looked different,
I dressed different,
I talked different,
I walked differently,
and for once
I could finally look at my reflection again.
My first-time, feeling self-confidence from head to toe.

If we don't conquer our mental battles,
If we don't overcome our greatest enemy...ourselves,
If we do not nurture ourselves, with self-love and forgiveness,

Then our TRUTHS and Trials
can manifest into DIS-EASE.

*We will no longer have control,*
*and we will give up our power.*
*Until, a conscious change is made*
*Healing cannot fully occur."*
*-Giovanna*


*Notebook Time:*

*The key to taking your power back,*
*is by taking control of everything you ingest.*

*Your self-talk: What do you say?*

*Your foods: What are you eating? Is it healing or is it making you sick?*

*Who do you spend most of your time around?*

*What do you spend most of your time doing?*

*What do you spend your money on?*

*Where do you want to go?*

*Who do you want to be?*

*Do you have a desired destination?*

*Are you working towards that direction? Or are you going in the opposite direction?*

*Wherever you are it's ok, let's locate you, and plug in a new destination.*


**This is the whole identity changer,
because it's about finding your true identity;
...... under it all.
Under, the negative talk,
Under, negative habits.
Beneath, the surface and down to the core.**

---

*There's blessings in our TRUTH's
and clarity, in our struggle.*

---

Affirmation:

I allow my life to flow
I allow my life to grow
I am blessed
I am grateful
I am protected
I am powerful
It's time
Here I am 11.11
I am ready universe.

# CHAPTER 18

## *Dear younger self*

> *"Trust and believe you are someone special,*
> *Someone unique, someone who is going to make a difference"*
> *-Giovanna*

In my teens and early adult years,
I've went through struggle, physically, mentally and spiritually.
Only to find the answers and purpose behind it all,
after, I had gone through the process.

*It felt as if I was given a test, with the teacher knowing I would probably fail,*
*after I was graded, I was then, taught the lesson.*

**With age comes understanding,**
**and with failure comes lessons.**

*Growing into self,*
*I see it literally, it makes sense, it's clear,*

---

*when we make the choice, to claim responsibility for our actions,*
*we can start to understand, the lesson rather than repeating the mistake,*
*and never moving forward.*
*That is when the cycle shifts off of repeat.... on to the next lesson and test :)*

---

At any age, especially as teenagers,
there are so many things we must learn,
unlearn, relearn and face on our own.
Things that we were never told, or prepared for,
but we will still be tested on.

*It feels like being stranded on a deserted island alone,*
*Dehydrated and hungry,*
*And you have no idea how to survive.*

Life can be ugly, and as we grow older, it doesn't get any easier.

**However, we gain our strength, by learning, and finding our power, when we are in the process of re-teaching ourselves how to survive.**

*We have to remember we have infinite wisdom within us.*

There is power in our tongue, and in our mind.

How do we expect to appreciate happiness?
*If we have never felt unhappiness?*

How do we expect to appreciate peace?
*If you have never encountered chaos?*

How do learn your body can heal itself?
*If you do not have an illness to cure?*

We have to experience comparison,
We have to doubt, and then witness miracles.
Tables turn, when you realize you are the miracle.

To dislike something, is truly only gained through experience.
How do you know what you deserve, if you do not experience the opposite?

Through learning these lessons,
we become one step closer to finding,
own enlightenment and power.

*It's a rubix cube puzzle and we are the cube,
being twisted and turned, in what we feel is random directions, for the
sole purpose of connecting the colors.*

In chaos there is clarity,
Only with trial and error is the game completed.

When we experience both,
*we can relate it with the opposite,
learning cause and effect.*

Sometimes, we can't appreciate the blessings,
Until we go through the lessons and complete a few chapters.

Starting small and expanding,
so that when we do receive our tremendous, life-changing blessings,
we've grown into who we've needed to become.

Strong enough, both mentally, and physically,
to receive all we've been asking for.

Growing through the process, we become humbled;
we learn who we are and who we are not,
eventually realizing we've been preparing for this.

There is no rushing the process,
Speeding up the seasons, is impossible.
Enjoy each page, of your book,
appreciate each season and
soak in the lessons each chapter brings.

It's no wonder so many suffer from depression, and feel alone,
We've given our power away,
or in truth, it was taken from us, over the years,
and we don't remember, how life works!
We haven't made a connection with self,
we don't think we have a voice, a choice and,
we forgot, that we can speak.

Like a baby bird leaving the nest,
we are forced to learn, and by being FORCED,
we recognize spirit,
and witness the power,
our power, we have wings to fly.

We see the cause and effect,
we also start to see the blessings.
As we start to focus, and refine our vision,
we notice our thinking was usually upside down.

*What we thought we couldn't do,*
*We were just too scared to try.*

*"I am no longer afraid to let go,*
*because I know what I'm letting in,*
*is bigger than what I am letting go."*
*-Giovanna*


*Affirmation:*

*I release all that holds me back from my purpose,*
*I forgive myself for all the mistakes I've made,*
*I let go of the person I no longer am,*
*and I allow the light to shine through me*

*Dear Younger self,*
*Let go of the pain,*
*Let go of the heartache when you were younger and didn't know.*
***The mistakes were lessons,***
***you pain, turned into a strength***
*You are ok,*
***you are safe now,***
*You are happy,*
*you are loved,*
*I affirm my greatness*
*To my younger self*
*It's ok*
*You were growing and learning*
*I love you*

*Say it with me,*
*I can achieve all things,*
*I must decide what I want, and take it!*
*I must step up, so that I can level up,*
*I am Possible*

*Affirmation:*

*I am possible*
*I am healing*
*I am growing*
*I am a co-creator*
*I am powerful*
*I am magick*
*I am enlightened*
*I am at peace in the present moment*
*I am surround by love, and abundance*
*I am grateful*

# CHAPTER 19

## *Frozen in fear*

> *"We are just creating stagnant time between our destiny,*
> *while patching voids in our own happiness."*
> *-Giovanna*

Happiness doesn't have to start when you get a new job,
get a raise, get straight A's, graduate, get accepted,
or even when you are loved.

> **Happiness starts,**
> **when you**
> **ALLOW**
> **YOURSELF**
> **to love yourself,**
> **unconditionally.**

AS YOU grow up and glow up!

> I have a message to tell you,
> just in case no one told you,
> it's ok to fail,
> Everyone makes mistakes.

It's never too late to start fresh and try again.

> No one is perfect,
> Life is full of misunderstanding, and regret,
> that doesn't have to hold you back, from being the best version of yourself. :)
> I think, no let me change that,
> I *know* my greatest setback and hold up,
> was my mind.

I was the one protecting me, from my greatest fear
my ultimate self!
*I had to give myself permission to be my raw, authentic self,*
to use my talents and abilities and finally,
share my words, wounds, and truths with the world.

## *YOU GOTTA RECHARGE YOUR CONFIDENCE, JUST LIKE YOU WOULD RECHARGE YOUR PHONE, DAILY*

*I've made mistakes,*
*I've had regret,*
*I've felt pain,*
*I've had heartache,*
*and because of all of that,*
*I am who I am today!*

*I AM stronger*
*than I ever would have been,*
*because of my struggles and trials.*

*It filtered the toxic people in and out of my life.*

*The important thing is to remember, **everything happens for a reason**.*

*There will always be a message, hidden in a mess.*

*I am here to tell you about the things,*
*I've learned along the way,*
*and all that it takes to be the best version of yourself.*

*Life is not easy, and anyone who has told you that, knows that's not true.*
*You may not be able to change what you're going through right now,*
*but you can always change the approach, in how you look at it.*
*(Yes, I know easier said than done)*

Personal growth, is forever growing,
forever evolving,
breaking, shattering and healing.
There is no right or wrong way,
but there are always ways to get there faster, and with less drama.

When you realize your true value,
you won't feel the need to conform, or confirm with your peers.
You will know your worth,
and if they can't see it, well then, they are too cheap for you.
They may get mad at this newly found self-love,
but that's only because, they can't afford you.

*This same mindset can be used in all aspects of your life.*
*When, you truly love yourself, and are happy with yourself,*

*life seems to flow easier.
You thaw out your fear,
You begin to drain out the drama,
You start to heal the conflict, and you learn,
you can revive, your own spirit.*

*Notebook Time:*

*What are some of the things that scares the crap out of you?*

*Now reread your answers, and ask yourself why am I scared of that?
How can you overcome your fears?*

*Are you scared of failing?
Have you tried? You can never succeed if you never try.*

*Are you scared of falling in love?
Have you been hurt? Are you scared to be vulnerable?*

*Are you scared of starting a new venture?
Ask yourself why? Do you not feel qualified, or worthy?
Read and learn how to be successful so you can be confident in your skills.*

# CHAPTER 20

## When the enemy is you

*"Bound with human excuses,
we know what our soul craves, but we allow fear to hold us back,
from going after our divine calling."*
-Giovanna

---

*We will never become who we were meant to be,
if doubt exists within ourselves, and controls our mind.*

---

*soak that in because if you don't believe in yourself, no one else will.
\*reread\**

I've learned one fundamental lesson,
with 3 keys factors, that we all should learn on this journey of life.

Can you guess what it is?

It's about **believing** in yourself, even when no one else does.

It is about **becoming** your best friend, rather than your worst enemy.

And finally, **Being** yourself, your beautiful raw, unapologetic authentic soul.

You guessed it,

**Self-love.**


Self-Love is
learning and having a healthy,
respectful, loving relationship with yourself

Knowing your true authentic value, and being grounded,
and rooted, in yourself.
Knowing you possess power and strength within,
you are a co-creator and healer.

*Why is it so hard, when it seems so easy?*
Because this isn't what we are taught, reminded, or encouraged to do,
we have an outdated program running on repeat in our head.
"I am stupid, I can't, I am not able to, I don't know how, I don't want to."
With negative toxic self-talk and all of this internal questioning,
it would make anyone question and devalue themselves.

*I understand, why you've questioned, because I use to question as well.*

As we grow through life, we come across these lessons,
eventually, webbing together, to create a spider web,
connecting it all together

We have to control our mind,
what we think becomes our reality.
Don't let it scare you,
let it excite you!
You hold the power!
There is amazing power in the words you speak,
Law of attraction.
Start using it in your favor.

*It's so backward,*
*We love others, more than we ever loved ourselves,*
*We listen to what others say,*
*But fail, to recognize, or listen,*
*to our gut, and intuition.*

We must release, Fear, pain, anxiety,
and make room, for hopes, and dreams, that turn into goals, and reality.

*All of our success, and failure, is a result of our mindset,*
*control what you think, and say, and change your life today!*

Lift your head beautiful,
today is a new day,
walk with spirit, and you will never be led astray.
Feel part of a bigger picture, and you will soon see,
your true potential and who you were meant to be

*Notebook Time:*

*Who is your biggest enemy and why?*
*If not an enemy, who is holding you back from your potential and ultimate happiness?*

*When you answer questions like this,*
*it gets your brain thinking, we also begin to look at it from a different angle.*
*By asking the question "who is my biggest enemy?" In writing the answers down, we see in black and white, who it is, and we can dissect and dig up the reason why they are your enemy.*
*From there, we can mentally, understand why, and begin to find our own personal freedom from our enemy, also known as our teacher.*

# CHAPTER 21

## Silently trying to starve out my imperfections

*trigger warning

> "We all struggle with our self,
> some can hide it better than others,
> I used to struggle,
> with keeping my smile on, and my scars and razor blade hidden"
> -Giovanna

I've struggled with depression, self-hate, and anorexia.

It's sad, that we learn to hide our true feelings, pain, and emotions,
because it makes others uncomfortable.
Or, we could be surrounded by people,
who just don't care, family, sometimes being the biggest one.

We lose hope in healing, because no one understands.

No matter what their opinion or belief,
that does not take away from the very real,
pain, and suffering, you are going through.

It is valid! It is real! It hurts!
You may not feel strong today love,
but the fact that you got out of bed,
the fact, you got dressed,
shows your resilience!
You showed up.

You're not ready to give up; you are a fighter!
Don't sell yourself short,
and don't feel incomplete, for being incomplete lol
You are whole; you are mighty, you are a survivor!
Put down the knife, and allow your body to heal,
wear your scars with pride,
they show the battles you've faced and survived!

*There is no way to fully understand, until you've fallen into that dark unknown yourself.*

---

**This pain, it can't be healed instantaneously, wished away or forgotten.**

Welcome to my emotional roller coaster
*want to take a ride?*

**It started in Middle school,**
*believing lies as truths, and drowning in the ups and downs of school;*
it turned into constantly self-hating myself and finding ways to cope.

**High school;**
*My silent years of hell, that turned into physical self-hating,*
I enjoyed cutting to release, and physically, seeing my pain bleed out of me.
It was my little secret.
I had a major break down, right before senior graduation, suicide watch,
recovered but never healed.
*Out of sight, out of mind, right?*
I eagerly continued, and packed, without looking back,
traveling thousands of miles away from the only home I knew.

**Off to college,**
*seeking something different,*
*a connection to find myself.*
Who was I?
Protecting my wounds, but eager to meet others
I eagerly walked into the next chapter of my life,
thinking this one, had to be better.

**In deep unknown waters;**
*My weaknesses were used against me,*
*my self-doubt, self-hate, manipulated in their favor,*
*my kindness taken, and abused,*
wrong decisions were made, as I connected with the wrong group of friends.
It felt like I was being flushed down the toilet,
was I going to drown?

**The second year,**
*they could smell my blood in the water*
I was a snack, placed in housing with 3 of the wrong roommates,
I sunk into my own darkness, while portraying a happy life to the
outside world.

**Dropping out early**

*I took a step forward, starting to speak my truths,*
*about who I was, and what made me happy.*
*But who I was, and my truths, and happiness,*
*did not match up and did not want to be heard.*

I become closed out, and dismissed, by my family,
for years after, moving back closer to home.
I moved forward though, we got our own place, and we started our life's as adults.

**Early 20's**
*I thrived for 4 years, but at a price, my mental disease.*
The disempowering environment,
the strive for physical perfection,
I was putting on a smile, while going through a constant state of self-hate, and comparison.
It paid very well, but it was not happiness

**Mid 20's**
*I covered up my insecurities with bad habits and bad decisions.*
Spinning out of control, and dealing with health issues,
I began to starve myself, physically.
I had moved past the physical cutting, and on to the food withdraw.
I was so unhappy, and if I couldn't control my reality,
I would damn sure control when and what I ate.

**This is when my 6-year eating disorder started.**
*At first, it was control, and to look a certain way,*
*that helpless thought that if you reached a certain weight,*
*you would feel better about yourself or gain control of your life.*
*But in all reality, it was so much deeper than that.*
**It became a constant habit, an addictive drug,**
**self-medicating, I yearned for.**
I had never been confident, this was just the thing
I needed to tip over in the wrong direction.
Suffering body dysphoria,
literally striving/starving for perfection on the outside
and totally neglecting my inside.

*In between, trying to gasp for air,*
*I suffered alone,*
*no one to talk,*
**no real friends, and not yet my own friend,**
*I fell into depression.*

As I literally, started to fade away,
I also began to get sick,
with aches and pains and constant flu-like symptoms.

They were unable to diagnose me for over a year,
my whole body was attacking itself.
Finally, answers,
I was positive, for ANA, an autoimmune disease.

**Late 20's**
*I went through an entire year, in indescribable chronic pain.*
All I could do was lay on the couch and pray God would take me.
Flares, where I was unable to use any part of my body, my joints throbbed, and my ligaments tighten and loosened like a rubber band.
I would cry when move,
I would cry when I couldn't.
I had to be carried to the bathroom.
No appetite and no energy to do anything,
this was my ultimate low.
I could barely wake up, let alone maintain, any relationships with anyone.

*I was a burden, and I had a pain, that could not be taken away.*

*It was there that I began,
to start my long journey,
befriending the beast...myself.*

**Beginning with self-doubt,**
**believing lies,**
**your mind becomes a mental mind battle,**
**Causing and inflicting physical pain on your own body.**


*Until, we are taught self-coping, self-help, and self-empowering tools,
until we learn, we must nurture our soul and soil with self-love,
we won't be able to get a decent crop.
Sowing the wrong seeds, using the wrong soil,
will not get the desired results.*

*We will always fall for triggers, if, we do not get to the roots.*

# CHAPTER 22

## Let's start a conversation

*Trigger warning

> *"I know it seems impossible, but this burden you are carrying
> is not yours to carry anymore"*
> *-Giovanna*

Let me continue to be open and honest,
I write this in loving memory for anyone who has lost the battle of mental illness,
for the families of loved ones who were left behind, and
for the beautiful broken souls
still fighting their ultimate battle within.
The battle is not over yet! Don't give up.

**In darkness, there is peace,
In peace, there is clarity,
In clarity, there is liberation.**

---

*Let's start a conversation, let's sit down, and talk about life,
this chapter is about our deep dark secret truth's;
Depression, suicide, and self-harm.*

---

So many suffer in silence,
all ages, males, and females
alone, afraid, anxious, discouraged, depressed and confused.

This silent killer,
this indescribable pain,
it's not talked about until,
the damage seeps out and affects others.

We allow others to suffer in silence,<br>
as long as it is not affecting us,<br>
if it is, we downplay, and brush off.<br>
Ignoring the core issue,<br>
that they are dying, from the inside out.

But depression. is a very real,
and it is a very scary reality for many,
it is a constant state of being.

It is not as easy as flipping a switch,
It's not as simple as wishing it away.

>It is the feeling of dying daily, but never finding peace.

>It is wanting to fly, but already feeling buried alive.

>It is like gasping for air and holding your breath.

>Fighting to breathe, and at the same time, wanting to take your last breath.

Depression and self-harm,
are two topics very few like to talk about,
and almost no one wants to talk about.

It's too sad, too "depressing."
It doesn't make sense; it's not that serious,
It makes me look weak; it's too uncomfortable.

*As you are battling the war within,*
*the war outside continues,*
*the pain continues,*
*and the stress piles up.*

>I've been a prisoner in that same darkness,
>I have wrestled with that same question,
>what is the purpose of life?
>While contemplating how and when.
>I've even written my own suicide note.

>I guess, I had to be taken to the edge,
>and helped off, so that I too, could help others off the ledge.
>I never understood my pain had a real purpose,
>until many years after.

After all of this,
I am still here,
I did not die.
Although I wished I had a few times.

I didn't think I was strong enough,
to live or die,
but in the back of my mind,
I really wanted someone to save me.

It wasn't my time,
I still had things I had to do.

I just wanted help,
Help from my own self.
I needed to be saved.
I couldn't understand,
I was in pain, and no one could see.
I was internally bleeding,
and no one even cared.

*Would they only notice after, I wasn't there to be missed?*

**My life is a present, in the present moment,**
and I have healed that broken or misunderstood part of me.
It is, and always will be part of my story, I do not hide it in shame.
Above all,
It is part of my strength,
It is part of my victory.

I conquered, defeated, and befriended,
the biggest enemy,
Myself.
**I overcame, my internal war,**
**I was able to save myself.**
*This story does not always end the same.*

For every survivor, there are 5 angels taken home,
For every healed there are 5 broken families.

**The tables turn, when you have to experience this kind of darkness,**
**or loss in your life, first hand.**

Your life changes forever,
you will never be the same,
How could you?
But, with this life changing experience,
there still is, purpose, and hope.

For the ones who have been left behind, by their loved ones,
you may never find all answers you are looking for, or the reasons
why.

But why would you want to?

*You know now deep down, that your loved one was in deep pain,*
*and is no longer is.*
*They have freedom, from their demons, and angel wings to fly.*

***There is peace in that statement.***

It is time, to cherish the memories,
embrace, the good times, and help others try to understand,
and heal from this deadly disease.
With your first-hand experience, you gain deeper understanding,
acknowledgement, and a deep compassion,
that no book could ever explain.

*A special message,*

*To the broken,*
*you are not broken, don't give up.*
*I care, I love you,*
*I know it, feels like you are suffocating, and*
*no one cares,*
*but I care, don't give up, it's not your time.*

*Together, we will get through this, one day,*
*one hour at a time.*
*There is great strength is fighting!*

To the ones left behind,
my heart goes out to you,
for the tears and pain, you now carry.
I pray, one day, you can find comfort, peace,
and understanding in your journey.

To the fallen, my beautiful soul, you are dearly missed,
but I rejoice in knowing you are now finally out of pain and in peace.

*3 different sides of the same story*
*it's time, we all started to have more compassion,*
*share more understanding,*
*and start a conversation.*

No one is perfect, and we all can relate to feeling alone.
Let us strive to help others in need,
rather than wait until,
it's too late.

Under that scared person contemplating his/her last breath,
is also broken soul, praying to be saved.

Hey you, yes, you!
Hold on!
Don't let go,
it's not time.
Don't give up,
You talk, I'll listen,
let's start a conversation.
You still have gifts within you,
you still have greatness flowing
through your blood.
Don't give up,
it's not your time.
It's time to be brave,
it's time to move forward,
it's time to keep going,

---

*It's time to befriend the beast instead of getting eaten by it.*

---

We can help heal the broken by,
giving compassion, and sharing, understanding.

In loving memory of a dear friend who lost the battle,
but now is in peace, and whole once more.
A dedication to his life and the wonderful family
he left behind.
You are missed.
You are loved.


Notebook Time:

Write whatever comes to mind, you have a blank page,
use it.


1-800-273-8255

# CHAPTER 23

## *Message received*

*"Pushed out of the nest, we learn we have wings to fly."*
*-Giovanna*

It is time;
to believe in your higher self,

it is time;
to believe in your own ability,

it is time;
to believe in your gifts,

it is time;
to believe in your strength,

it is time;
to believe you are still alive for a reason,

it is time;
now is the time,
to pursue your happiness, your purpose, and your goals!

*Cheat sheet*

---

*You will find your inner strength,*
*usually during, not before,*
*but while going through, your struggle.*

---

You will eventually discover your own internal compass,
also known as your gut instinct.
Listen to it, befriend it, and let it guide you.

*If life is all about showing up,*
*and the key is faith.*
*Half of the battle is coming into agreement,*
*and believing it is possible.*

When effort meets passion,
and talent, meets the stage,
magic will always be seen.

It is not about having the money,
it is simply believing.
You first must believe that you are special and deserving.
Dream big and know you are worthy of it.

*You are a star,*
*shining bright*

**\*\*Do you get the picture, you are Magic\*\***

*Believe me, in the beginning, and even during, it doesn't make sense.*

We are still thinking logically,
looking at everything like it needs to make sense,
but what is faith?
Believing, in something you cannot physically see.

*Could it be that easy?*
*SEEK my T.R.U.T.H.S,*
*and I will START to find my healing?*

We can use every excuse in the book;
*I don't know how, I have the worst life, I can't, I have the negative mindset,*
*I am sick, I hate myself, I'm broken, I'm broke, I'm too old, I am too young,*
*no one believes in me, and this list can go on.*

I used to make a lot of excuses, and
I did a lot of questioning, doubting, and running in fear too.

I waited for others approval,
seeking acceptance.

*I thought I had to have it all together;*
*I thought I needed to have all the answers.*
*I thought I had to be perfect, and know what to do next,*

*But I didn't, and I don't.*

There are signs everywhere, angel messages, or spirit messages,
guiding us, coming to us all the time in numbers, or synchronicities,
(*license plates, prices, receipts, etc.*) showing themselves through
advertisements we see, or hear, posters, billboards, company names,
symbols, movies, songs, basically, any form of communication,
including a person or a book.
Everything is connected, for the good of all.

                Lessons will be learned,
                knowledge will be gained,
      and blessings, will be received, and given.

*Once we learn this, it's almost like,*
*The beginning of a transformation.*

You see, think, act, and say, things differently.

          *You realize, there is a greater power,*
              *and you possess that power,*
         *and with power, comes responsibility,*
             *as well as promotion.*

*Meditate,*
*on your God-given path,*
*Pray and revisit your gifts.*

                  *Remembering,*
                  *who you are,*
            *IS THE GAME CHANGER*

*Let the universe clear the way,*
it's not your responsibility to know how, it all will happen.

              **You've just got to trust.**
        **If you are uncomfortable trusting,**
                  *ask yourself why?*

*Why do you lack trust?*
*Is it an old mentality, or way of thinking?*
Or
*is your gut trying to talk to you?*

*Is it trying to show you something?*
Try to listen, is it how you have been treated,
respected, or disrespected?

*Do you know you deserve more?*
But, you've been playing it safe,
scared to make changes.

*Well until we decide to change,*
*We will stay in the same spot.*


*Literally, until you tell someone to stop hitting you,*
*Will they stop?*
*You must speak up and tell them to stop!*


*We need to believe, we are worth more*
*than our current situation.*
*We must start looking for what we do want, what we deserve.*


*Notebook Time:*

*Start to look at your surroundings,*
*notice the subtle signs, from above,*
*pay attention to the repeating numbers,*
*and start to look up angel numbers meanings.*

*Have you seen any?*


*Look for the synchronicities,*
*look for answers, to the questions you ask.*

*Ask questions and listen to your intuition for guidance.*

# CHAPTER 24

## Why?

*"Allow yourself to dream bigger than the restraints, you put on yourself,
We are only limited in our own beliefs."*
-Giovanna

To succeed,
to reach your desired destination,
first, you need a target.

*Then, you need a reason why?*
The why, is what will keep you going.

What will give you strength when you want to give up?
Find your why,
and you will find your unlimited source of fuel.


Why?

*Why do I write?*
I am writing this book,
For myself;
As part of my own growth,
As part of my own healing,
As part of my own soul contract.


*In hopes, to find internal healing, and become a beacon of hope
for someone else, suffering in silence.*


I know what it is like to suffer, for years, in silence.
To not feel accepted, understood,
and to hate your reality, and even worse self.


We all have different journey's, but, similar obstacles to overcome.

I struggled and still struggling,
with myself.

*I love myself, and battle myself, all in the same day.*
*I am far from perfect,*
*I am a work in progress,*
*A masterpiece, and a beautiful, unfinished, piece of art.*

                    I have been hiding, in my own darkness,
                        drowning, in my own fear,
                        too weak, to move forward
                        and too, strong to let go.

My why, has never let me down.
My why, has saved me from quitting too early.
My why, is me,
My life, is no coincidence,
My pain, is no mistake,
My words, hold power,
They hold healing.

My purpose, is to share,
share with you my truths.
Share with you my pain, my power, my passion, and best of all,
my compassion.

                      *This is my life purpose,*
                *I am here to share with the world, who I am.*

                *My life is an offering to humanity.*

              My purpose, has always been to uncover my power,
                    unfold the hidden map,
                    and reveal it to you.
                    I am not just my story,
                    I am my own power source,
                    I am my own super hero.

*I used to be scared of my truths, my voice,*
*and worst of all, myself.*

I had to face my demons,
and I still do.

I struggle with self-love,
and have struggled many times, to be strong.

*But that is what created me*

That is what exposed the real authentic me.

All the trash I had to release,
let go, and work through,

The ugly truth,
about facing your reflection.

I am strong, because I had to be.
We can all relate.

But what makes us amazing, is that we didn't give up.
Against all odds, we are still here.

We always have issues, and stuff to deal with;
it's life, we evolve.

*When you can confidently, and authentically, be you,*
*that says something!!*

*That is true POWER,*
*Speak your truths,*
*Share your darkness,*
*Show your light,*
*You are part of the Divine.*

*Notebook Time:*

*Write out your whys?*
*Why are you in here?*
*What do you think your purpose is?*

*Don't know?*

*Start with your talents and work your way back,*
*What are you good at?*
*What makes you happy and gives you fulfilment?*

"Find the reason why, and you will always, have a reason to keep going."
-Giovanna

# CHAPTER 25

## *Mirage, Playing catch up*

> "When I was putting together this book,
> I started to read through all of my old notebooks, journal, and saved files,
> I realized I had been writing to my future self."
> -Giovanna

The next few chapters, I wanted to include to show you how we grow into ourselves;
usually our dreams sound crazy, and a lot happens in between
a dream and becoming a reality.

March 2015
We all have our battles,
some are physical, some are mental,
one thing is for certain;
we are all human,
and deep down inside
we have a beautiful soul.

**We grow up,**
**We learn,**
**We evolve,**
**We change,**

We all can be somebody,
we all can make a difference,
we can change our lives,
and be, whoever we want to be.

**Become motivated by defeat,**
**learn to love a good challenge,**
**become your own greatest enemy,**
**and defeat yourself, mind, body, and soul.**

Bring out your best,
push through the mental barriers that say you can't do this!

---

*Set goals for yourself, and beat them.*

---

Start somewhere, and little by little,
learn to set aside time for yourself.

Work on yourself!
Soon, you will be loving the feeling of your new-found growth.

> **At first, it feels uncomfortable,**
> **it's dark and lonely.**

It can be confusing, and frustrating,
everything around you seems way too much pressure to handle.

> **Don't worry; you are going through a process;**
> **you will start to lose friends;**

You may separate from people, who you thought you'd be with your
Whole life.
It is ok, sometimes, people are removed from our life to protect us.
Trust the process.

You may feel like you are getting deeper, and deeper, away from where
You should be, we all can take the wrong path; it's our own free will.

> **Sometimes it takes months, years, or even decades,**
> **until, we find we are going the wrong way.**

Suddenly, realizing you want to change?
*Go for it! Change!*

---

*You can always go in the other direction,*
*Just give yourself permission.*

---

We all make mistakes, and in return,
we learn our lessons.

We need to process what we learn, and go through
and keep it up there, mentally.

Because, we will always be tested, again, and again
just like with computers.

A test will always be run.
right before a system upgrade.

When that situation occurs,
take it head on.

You've been there, you've done that,
Be confident in your own abilities.

If you've succeeded or failed,
There is always a lesson or lessons to be learned, and knowledge to be gained.

Learn to grow, from every experience,
when it happens again, you need to remember,
you have been prepared for this.

You know now, you can take the different route,
you can take another path, explore have fun, and go on an adventure.

We can change at any point,
Boom! Just like that.

It will take dedication, to keep new habits,
but it's possible, and I encourage anyone, and everyone, to change and try it.

We all have little things that we want to change, or drastically improve on.
For me, I wanted to change my mentality.

---

*I had to clean out my internal hard drive so to speak,
and replace it with a newly updated version.*

---

*I couldn't go any farther with the system I had,
so, I did a huge overhaul.*

It was filled with a lot of breakdowns,
tears, anger, and finally, forgiveness

I came out a new me!
A stronger me!
A me I loved!
A me I believed in!

*Notebook Time:*

*One simple question*

*What do you need to give up, to get more of what you truly desire?*

*Is it bad habits? Addictions? Negative self-talk? Letting go of someone?*
*Changing your environment, job or attitude?*
*Or best of all is it your limited beliefs?*

# CHAPTER 26

## *Releasing and forgiveness*

*"Once we allow ourselves to let go of all the past emotions,
we can allow ourselves to release the baggage, we've been carrying.
This next destination your headed to, requires no baggage, just bring yourself!"*
*-Giovanna*

Shedding skin on a whole new level.
Sometimes, we must love ourselves so much,
that we let go of all we've ever known.

Let go of all the years of negative self-talk,
let go of how others saw, or see you,
release, and let go,
and make room for all that there is.
Become reborn into the universe of infinite beings

Learning to let go,
even if there was no apology for the pain,
releasing is your way of reclaiming your power.

Their presence has left,
but the pain remains....

It's ok, learn from that experience,
acknowledge the pain,
and release it.

---

*Let it go, and fill yourself up with
some of that good self-love.*

---

It's time,
there's a shift,
I feel it.

Like the seasons changing,
death and birth.

There is life in all

*It's time we started to get less distracted,
and more focused.*

**Repeated section, in case you forgot,**

It's time to do less blaming,
and more forgiving self

*It's time, to let go of the pain,
let go of the heartache,
let go of it all, for personal freedom.*

*You do not have to justify the pain,
you do not have to justify the anger*

But you will only be all of this,
if that is all you let in.

You will always be in pain,
if that is all you focus on and seek.

Especially, when you leave no room for any other emotion,
like peace, hope and healing.

---

*You don't have to continue the years of pain, after the battle.*

*You don't have to keep fighting a war, that was meant never to be fought.*

---

Put down the sword
Put down the knife
It's ok you are safe
You are protected

When you push past your comfort zone,
and tap into your past emotions, wounds and internal damage,
you can find the purpose,
and finally heal.

*Affirmations:*

*I affirm I am on my way towards living my best life*
*I affirm my freedom to dream big and be happy*
*I allow myself to heal by letting go of the past*
*I allow the pain of yesterday to be released*
*And make room for the greatness that is already on its way to me.*

# CHAPTER 27

## Law of attraction

> *"Your mind is your greatest asset, start using it in your favor, rather than using it against you."*
> *-Giovanna*

Life is good, when we think it's good.
Life is bad, when you think it's bad.
Keyword, THINK.

---

*Create the best day,*
*by affirming exactly, what you want to see.*

---

Feed your mind with thoughts of abundance, peace, and love.
In a world where we can't control much,
one thing we have 1000% control of is our thoughts.

**Change your reality, by changing the way you think, and your self-talk.**

What are you ready for?
What are you waking up early and staying up late for?
What are you constantly thinking about?
What are you focused on?

What are your constant thoughts?
*That is what you are drawing to you.*

**Make sure what you focus the most on,**
**is really, what you want to see.**

*Focus on success, draw in success,*
*Focus on lack, stay in lack.*

Let me ask you again,
What are you ready for?!

**You are in control,
and if you don't feel in control,
it's time to take control.**

You must change your way of thinking,
and learn to control your own mind.

Tell yourself that you are going to make it,
even if you don't believe it.

You're going to make it,
you've got this,
all is well.

You are a money magnet,
You are successful,
You easily manifest your desires.

New moon
New intentions
New outcomes

**We have control over our thoughts,
just like we have control over what we put into our bodies.**

We have a choice;
*but the lazy and easy way, is auto programming and junk food.*

You must make a choice, to eat healthy,
the same goes for making a choice towards working on positive self-talk.

**Fill yourself with wonderful self-talk, and organic veggies today.**

*We are responsible for how other people treat us,*
*and they might not like this new me*
But oh well,
I know, I'm worth it.

*Empower yourself daily,*
*You know you deserve better!*
*Be grateful and open to all of the abundance*
*that your present and future hold.*

*If you only believed you are worth it!*

We are just beginning the best part of our life,
with all the ups and downs that have happened,
have compassion, and <u>understanding for yourself,</u>
Give love, support, and gratitude, for how far you've come.

**Celebrate the little victories,**
**and remember you have infinite power within.**
**Get ready, get ready!**

---

*It is all about your mindset.*

---

**It's never too late**
**to do a system overload,**
**delete trash, and realign, and refocus.**

*Notebook Time:*

*Quick thought,*
*answer the question below.*

*What is the majority of your thoughts?*

*Do you find yourself saying;*
*I don't have, I can't, I don't know to, I will never be able to, I'm broke, I don't have money for that, I am too stupid, I won't be able to,*
*Remember what you focus on, you attract.*

*Imagine if you constantly thought;*
*I am able, I am abundant, I am smart, I am victorious, I am determined, I am strong, I am a wealthy*
*I am an opportunity magnet!*

*repeat after me;*

*WE CREATE OUR OWN REALITIES.*

*SERIOUSLY!*
*Right now, today get a hold of your thoughts.*
*Stop the negative mindset and auto responses.*
*Write down what you do want!*
*Focus on it, revisit it constantly.*
*Have those thoughts on repeat,*
*Like your favourite song in your head*

*I can create my best life, and it starts today with me!!*

*Today keep telling yourself,*
*I GOT THIS!!!*

*It might feel funny at first, but I guarantee results in your life.*
*Why?*
*Because you are starting to believe in yourself, and you have taken control over what you want to see, and you have been empowered to let go and release, that which you no longer want!*

*YOU'VE GOT THIS!*
*I believe in you*
*xoxo*

# CHAPTER 28

## *Be you without making excuses*

*"Sometimes, your humbleness, makes others forget how much of a savage you are inside.
Don't be afraid to be your true authentic, beautiful self!
The world needs more authentic souls like you."
-Giovanna*

It doesn't matter if anyone likes you,
It doesn't matter if they "get you."
The key, is that you love yourself
The rest is irrelevant,
Shine bright loves.

It's true the guilt is real,
but we must learn to say no,
and not feel guilty, for protecting our energy.

We must learn, to give ourselves permission to do all the things we did for others,
for ourselves, without feeling guilty.
It's not wrong to say no,
it's not wrong to put yourself first.
If you don't no one will?

*I tried to find my identity in society,
instead of finding my identity within.*

**Sometimes you need to be misunderstood,
to understand yourself.**

Everyone saw me as a kitten
when I've always been a lioness.

*Notebook Time:*

*Have you been held back by someone else's opinion of you?*

*What did they say? Who was it?*

*Did you mistakenly identify with their opinion of you?*
*Feeling less than, dumb, ugly, doubtful, or embarrassed?*

*Do you feel stuck where you are because you believe you are unable to accomplish it?*

*It is time to rewrite who you are, create a list of 20 qualities that you possess,*
*What makes you unique?*
*What sets you apart?*

*It's time to show yourself some love.*

# CHAPTER 29

## Self-love, eating organically

*"Time to be all about yourself,
for yourself, and learn to feed yourself,
no guilt,
only organic self-love."
-Giovanna*

I've been guilty of it, but I'm here to tell you,
It's never too late, to learn to love yourself again,
It's never too late, to forgive yourself, for mistakes, and past pain.

It is too late to change the past,

Feel empowered,
that you can change the future.

That's all that matters,
Meet yourself with compassion and understanding.

SELF LOVE has become an endangered species,
and I'm here to save this beautiful wildlife!
Will you help me?
I am not giving up,
I will give hope,
as SELF, we are a beautiful, unique, divine being,
we shouldn't hide the statistics,
We've become domesticated.
We are killing ourselves off,
because we forget how to feed our own soul.

Imagine meeting OURSELVES,
shouldn't we be our ultimate desire?
Our Biggest fantasy, and predestined soul mate?

**We need to get intimate, with our SOULS!**

**We need to remember, how to love ourselves.**

*Only through understanding, and forgiveness,*
*can we ever understand ourselves,*
*and learn to love others again.*

                          I have
             understanding from my experiences,
              compassion from my pain,
              and wisdom from my darkness.

              Let me reveal myself to you,
               showing you my unfiltered,
              broken, and most intimate self.

                *How deep and honest*
               *will you get with yourself?*

Fall in love with yourself, your soul, your yoni, your body, your being. touch yourself, make love to yourself.

---

*Becomes your deepest desires, and connect passionately,*
*with all of your beauty.*

---

Become addicted to your own essence,
your own voice, your own smell, fall in love so passionately,
that the only one you need, is you.

           **Make love with your soul and feel the connection.**

*Nourished, and grounded,*
*connected and yet from another world.*

                     *Notebook Time:*

         *When was the last time you wrote a letter?*

           *It is time, to write yourself a love note,*
               *get intimate, get in detail.*

       *Share a deep, intimate, secret conversation*
         *with yourself, call yourself out by name,*
*start to crave your own energy, instead of seeking someone else's.*

             *You are exactly what you need.*

# CHAPTER 30

## Becoming me

> *"I guarantee whatever you heard about me,
> is diluted version of who I really am"*
> -Giovanna

I value my time,
and I've started to reassess how I spent it,
and what I spent it on.

Less talking,
more meditating.

Less stressing,
more gratitude.

Less makeup,
more soul work.

---

*Change can only happen, when you let go of something, sometime, that is your flawed perception of yourself.*

---

Everyone I meet, will see me differently,
that's ok.

*You meet me at your level of perception,*
too salty, too sweet, depending on your taste, not mine.

I'm not here to feed your appetite,
I'm not a snack to your soul.

*I'm not here to be understood,*
and I know I definitely won't be loved by all.
I'm here to heal, grow, and flourish.
I'm here to make mistakes and learn!

*I'm here to live, and lead, by example, of being a high vibrating old soul,
re-learning her magic day by day. helping others.*

One foot in front of the other,
two steps forward, one step back.
No longer caring whose feathers I ruffle,
It's time I spread my wings,
and became my deepest desire.

*The day I fell in love with myself,
was the day my whole life changed.*

No more watering down my awesomeness,
even if you wanted to.

You can't drown a lotus,
we grew in the mud.

I've been planted for a long time, it's my season,
It's time to see me open up and blossom.

2018 was the first year,
I chose to be my own best friend,
instead of being my worst enemy.

My life has been changing ever since.
I set goals, and I've achieved them,
I see it's POSSIBLE,
I can speak things into existence.

I have always had power,
but I've been tripping over myself, for years,
holding myself back,
narrating my own nightmare.

Now, is the time!
Step into your purpose,
Harness your magic,
it is time, to celebrate your growth!

Dance in your darkness,
and thrive in the unknown.

It's time to find your own happiness,
create your own reality,
and CELEBRATE your success.

                    Cheers love,
        The only person you need on your team,
                       is you!
          The only support you need, is you.
                You are more than enough,
                     you are perfect,
                      you can do it,
                       I promise.

*The freedom, liberation, growth,*
*happiness, and peace that comes,*
*once we TRULY allow ourselves to break,*
*words can't even begin to describe!*


                I am on a relentless growth process,
                and with every tear, I feel lighter.

                        With every release,
                        I feel empowered!

If we accept the pain, we will not heal.
*How can we?*
If we accept it and do not ask it to leave?


                *But, if we feel the pain and release it,*
                    *we allow ourselves to let go,*
                    *and allow healing to occur.*


Honor your pain, struggle, and setbacks,
become empowered by knowing,
you have so much power within you.


                    *All of these setbacks,*
            *have been trying to bring out and show you,*
                   *just how amazing you are!*

It's harder trying to hold yourself together,
when you are broken,
rather than allowing yourself to break.

                    *I encourage everyone to break,*
                       *break down, break free,*
                      *BREAK, SO YOU MAY HEAL.*

We are on divine timing,
you are never late,
and you lack nothing.
With love,
Giovanna

*Go after your desires, passions,*
*and achieve your dreams,*
*don't let anyone stop you,*
*not even your own mind.*

**Self-love is the best love you can ever receive.**
**To love your reflection, is to liberate your soul.**

# CHAPTER 31

## *When your wings arrive*

> "At my rawest, I feel my most authentic,
> showing my true colors,
> I've found my element,
> I've found my voice,
> I found the universe,
> within me!"
> -Giovanna

You already know what you need to do,
it may scare the crap out of you,
*but do it anyway!*

**Take that leap of faith**

*Let me try and explain,*

after losing myself to others,
and after breaking,
and continuing to break,
I am starting to find my freedom.

By finding my purpose,
and speaking my truths,
I am starting to feel lighter,
and lighter, as the days pass.
I'm finding myself a little more,
I'm learning to say no,
I'm learning to rest,
I'm learning to love myself <u>unconditionally,</u>
I'm learning about myself, and my likes and dislikes,
I appreciate my journey, and I appreciate all the messenger's
I am meeting on the way.

> *"I can finally say with confidence,*
> *I know, I'm on the right path, inward.*
> **It's always been the desired destination,**
> **the strength to get there was gained, during the journey."**

Don't get it confused,
when we are growing, and realizing we are missing something,
it usually doesn't feel like a warm ray of sunshine,
more like standing in the desert with no shade in sight.

But trust the process,
know that if your life is turned upside down, chaotic,
or you feel like you're losing it,
heed the warnings,
now is the perfect time to mix it up and let go!

*Let the universe do the hard part, you just trust in the process!*

Now that I can say
This is me,
this is the stage I'm at,
that is a major accomplishment.

*I've battled myself, many years,*
*This year I broke free from my chains.*

I've pushed past my fears,
I fought off the fire-breathing dragon,
I channeled my inner beast,
and I am continuously working on my self-love muscles.
I am a warrior,
I am the divine,
I am perfectly imperfect,
I am me!

## I killed off excuses,
## Success, I'm coming for you now!

*Your life changes, when find the courage to overcomes your fears.*

Into the deep dark unknown I go,
Retrograde here I am,
Shed my skin,
Renew my purpose,
Push me into the next level.

I am coming out of my darkness,
I have just danced around my ashes,
I've let go of ego, and allowed my higher spirit in,
I am not for sale,
I am priceless,
I am magical,
I am a unique one a kind piece of art,
and so are you.

*We all are,
perfectly, imperfect,
graciously growing,
tried, and true.*

**Authentically, I stand tall,
for the whole world to see.**

*This is me,
no more apologies,
I am powerful.
Do you see me?
I am healing myself,
so that I may share my trials and encourage others to heal,
I lead by example.
We are all connected,
our journeys will cross.
We are all healing ourselves, to heal the world.*

Mirror work,
stand in front of the mirror and talk to yourself,
befriend the person you are staring at,
smile and call yourself out by name.
Speak life, and happiness, into
your mind, soul, and body.

---

*I broke up with fear,
and made up with self.*

---

I am focused,
I am aligned,
I am guided.

**We are here,
I am here,
as a collective.**

**Now is the time,
the shift has come,
the awakening has already begun.**

*No more excuses,*
it's time to celebrate, and give gratitude,
your ancestors are so proud of you.

Spirit is supporting us,
I speak into existence,
what, I want to see in my life.

I remind myself,
I am powerful,
I am mighty,
I am magical,
I am unique,
I am loved,
I am lovable,
I am healing,
I am spirit.

I make no more excuses,
hiding behind fear.
I dance in my purpose,
I celebrate my own success,
I am (insert name),
and I am here to change the world.

I am a mighty warrior,
I no longer questioning who I am.

No more hiding in fear of rejection.

I no longer make excuses,
it's too late for that.

I am no longer fearful of my purpose,
I accept my God given path.

I accept and love myself,
I am me, I am perfect.

I am everything I have ever needed,
I am a co-creator.

**SPEAK THESE AFFIRMATIONS OUTLOUD WITH BELIEF**

      I'm a new person,
      I think differently,
      I act differently,
      I live differently,
      I speak differently,
      I am different.
      I've accepted and moved forward,
      I've forgiven and let go.
      I am new because,
      I let go,
      I let go of my past,
      I let go of my mistakes,
      I let go of my regret,
      I let go of my judgment,
      I let go of my insecurity,
      I let go of my failures,
      and I made room for all that I do want!!

*I only focus on possibilities, and dreams!*
*I will, because I can.*

*You are the bridge,*
*You are the teacher, you've been seeking,*
*You are the answer, you've been praying for,*
*God*
*Angels*
*Universe*
*Ancestors*
*they've got your back*
*All is provided*
*You are protected*

# CHAPTER 32

## *Relationships*

> *"The world has enough enemies*
> *become your best friend."*
> *-Giovanna*

Why do we tell the younger generation that you should **accept poor dating habits**?
*"Deal with it, you won't find anything else out there."*

Why do we tell our younger generation that you need to **learn to settle**?
*"No one is perfect, do you want to always be single?"*

Why do you teach your daughters, to not worry if their boyfriend is **cheating on them**?
*"It's normal just accept it, everyone has someone on the side, get used to it."*

Or flip side telling our sons,
women will always **use you for money**,
at least make sure you get a hot one.

> **Why is it that kids are jumping into relationships,**
> **and left broken after the break-up?**
>
> ***Zero self-worth***

Why is it kids are not learning to love themselves?
*But mastering making others happy.*

Why are there so many kids dying with this silent pain?!
*Because, we aren't teaching them.*

Why do they keep making the same mistakes we made?
*Because, we aren't switching up the auto responses we tell them,*
*we are not updating our mindset and for the next generation,*
*we are not empowering them to change their self-worth.*

We aren't leading by example,
we need to change the script!
It's time, it's past time!

It's time, to not only act differently,
but BE different.

*Let's choose to live differently,*
*let's raise the standards and show our children,*
*you are strong for walking away!*

New priorities

Forget the designer clothes,
let's teach them about self-worth, self-love, and self-respect.
Your value does not depend on your shopping receipts.

Let's show them that it's ok to desire love, and commitment,
but, only first after finding it and giving it with ourselves.

Let's lift up our kids,
and let them know what it feels like,
to be loved unconditionally, and to know what love is.
So, they don't go seeking it from an outside source.

Let's dare to love, and respect, ourselves again!
No longer caring who we lose in the process!

Let's learn to forgive, and heal, without an apology,
let's take our power back!

*No more excuses,*
*they don't know, because we don't teach them!*
*It's time for a change!*

Be proud of yourself,
whatever stage of life you are at,
good or bad, ups or down,
Single, married, or divorced,
whether you like men or women, both or neither.

Remember to celebrate your awesome, amazing self!

*Are you worried because you don't have anyone?*
How many people who are reading this, are getting worried they
don't have someone?

*Time is moving, but you are still single?*

*Trust the process,*
*it's giving you time to give yourself,*
*the love you desire.*
*Rest assured,*
*you will meet up, in divine timing.*
*Now is the time, to love yourself,*
*So, you will be able to accept the love,*
*that you seek.*

Most seek relationships on a physical level,
they fall in love with outer appearance,
and don't even care to dive into the deep layers of their lover.

They fall for with what they see, anything physical,
and neglect the delight on the inside, the soul.

They don't love you,
they love your look, or how you make them feel.

*But how do they make you feel?*

**I seek in-depth soul on soul contact.**

*I want to be touched, not physically but spiritually and mentally.*

**The one thing you should lust after,**
**is not the physical connection,**
**but the divine, intimate spiritual connection.**

Anyone can have sex,
*but who feeds, fulfills and ignites your soul, with the fruits of endless*
*highly addictive love?*

*Love yourself first, so you know what the divine connection you seek feels*
*like.*

*Hit your spot, so you do not seek someone to do it for you.*

*Make love to yourself, so you know what the passion feels like.*
*Never again, settling for less.*

Think about it,

*Are you appreciated for your soul or your looks?*

*Are you loved for who you are or who they want you to be?*

*Who do they love? Do they even love themselves?*

*Do they connect with you or are you disconnected?*

**Do you love yourself enough to know when someone doesn't truly love you? Or, do you get scared, and allow it to go on, terrified of being alone?**

Remember my dear,
you are never alone, you will always have you!
Love yourself and set high standards.

You deserve the love you seek,
and guess what!?
You are worth it!
Now live like you want to be treated,
and you will soon match frequencies,
and connect with the right soul mate.

*Remember if you still need healing,*
you may find a partner who will help you grow in ways
you may not have asked for, or wanted,
but the end result is always what we needed or seek.

*Seek wisely,*

You are so amazing
and loved for being you!
***Even if no one has reminded you lately.***

No matter if you have someone or not,
you are loved and appreciated.
Do not judge your value based on a day, or what society says.

---

*You, my dear, are AMAZING*
*today, tomorrow, yesterday and every day.*

---

You've got this!
Speak life!
Speak strength, and healing!
Speak greatness and love over your life!
Remember, you are part of the Divine.
What you are seeking, is seeking you.


*Notebook Time:*

*Now is the time you have been waiting for,
time to practice your manifest skills.*

*Write out what you are looking for in a relationship.
What qualities do you want the love of your life to have?
Think beyond physical for a moment and focus on personality, likes and dislikes.*

*Once your list is completed,
If you are good at drawing, now you can draw it out, or with words describe,
Visualize
The look of your soul mate,
what color hair, eyes, body type, race, age.*

*Remember, just as you are making a list,
your soul mate is doing the same.
Not everything is physical, think deeper.*

*You get what you ask for.*

*Make sure you are available, and healed, before
you get into a relationship.*

# CHAPTER 33

## *Soul food*

*"Deep in my darkness,
I found my own buried treasure."
-Giovanna*

---

*The magnificent power, in forgiving self.*

---

I love and respect myself like never before,
I honor my wounds, and acknowledge my past,
as a fool that pushed me into the great unknown!

I embody my purpose,
and I stand tall and walk in my greatness,
with my head held high.

*I am a warrior, I've fought many battles,
But I have arrived at my crossroads, and now headed towards my purpose.*

I affirm power and healing over my life.
I am powerful
I am strong
I am a radiant Goddess
I am healed
I am a healer
I am a alchemist
I am the co-creator of my life
I am protected by Spirit,
I am empowered,
and I empower others to walk in their light and embody their truth.

Now, is the time,
to take the leap of faith.
Follow my lead,
let go of your fears,
and leave your doubts behind.

You are the answer,
speak life into your life
be your own soul food!!

Affirmation
I am so excited to be back in my alignment,
stepping into my purpose and dancing in my greatness!

I am grateful for the amazing connections and beautiful souls I've been connecting with!
I know without a doubt I am supported by Spirit and the Universe.

I've broken up with my fears,
and I'm dancing in my greatness.
I'm in love with myself,
and I am supported by the Great Divine,
we are all, co-creators.
Claim your power.

*Follow me,*
*and I'll have you starting to loving yourself.*
*No competition baby,*
*Only EMPOWERMENT!*

Affirm, your power and dance in your greatness.
We all need a friend,
we all need a motivator,
we all need ourselves.
That is who you want,
That is who you need,
You, need you!

*I am reflection,*
*I am a message.*
*You are your own knight in shining Armor,*
*your words have power,*
*spread love, support, and encouragement,*
*to all.*

*Let me get you high off life*

You've got this!
You are ready!
You've been prepared.
Do it,
take a leap of faith,
and trust in yourself,
and in the universe.
You are protected always.

# CHAPTER 34

## *Becoming your own superhero*

> *"It's time, to realize who you are!*
> *Don't fight it,*
> *all in your timing will you understand."*
> *-Giovanna*

I'm 31 years old,
and I've been depressed and happy,
suicidal and overjoyed,
sick and healthy,
self-hating and self-loving.

I speak my T.R.U.T.H.S
to show vulnerability and
to allow others to heal,
because we need to see, we're not alone.

We all have insecurities,
we all have flaws,
but it's time we all started embracing ourselves.

> We need to go within,
> and get reacquainted with our soul, to heal.
> Learning we needed every trial, and setback,
> to become the superhero, we are today.

*Signs and wonders are all around,*
*the channel and direct connection are there,*
*we just have to tune in and listen.*

> Trust the process,
> you are not going crazy,
> you are one of a kind,
> and desperately needed.

Let it go,
drop the dead weight,
and fly!

It's time to upgrade,
but you can't,
until you trade in your old mentality!

*Can you see the difference?*
I admit, I'm breaking,
I've been letting go of a lot of bs and pain,
cleansing, purging, and learning a lot about myself the last year.
It's like an annual cleanse,
the first step to healing,
is destruction of the old self.

I've been at work creating something new,
I've let go of how others saw me,
and I've stepped out of my comfort zone,
and started to living authentically.

*I've been finding who I want to be, not, who others wanted me to be.*

I've let my curls out, my hair down,
and embraced my imperfections, the lioness is here to stay.

I have come out of this battle a warrior.
My journey, has been full with ups and downs,
facing of my truths, and letting go of pain,
while sitting in my darkness.

*I've searched within, instead of seeking outward.*

I have always struggled with myself,
but I'm tired of fighting back and forth,
struggling to keep my own happiness.

This warrior will rise,
the monster will be defeated,
I am fighting the ultimate battle,
against myself.

I do not smile, 100 percent of the time, no one does.
But I'm working on being GIOVANNA,
100 percent of the time,
and that's all that matters!

Find yourself, and then fall in love with yourself,
you are your own super hero.

*I think, what scares someone the most,*
*is to question what they've known, what they've been taught, and who they've become.*
*To revisit their false truths,*
*and let go of the control they have been clinging on to.*

**But in releasing, realizing, they possess power**
**and infinite wisdom,**
**within.**

# CHAPTER 35

## *It's time, so start getting ready!*

> *"Your future depends on your actions,*
> *not anyone else's.*
> *You can wait, or you can go through the door and change."*
> *-Giovanna*

It's time to move on,
cut cords,
change numbers,
grow, and blossom.
*I let go and make no excuses.*
*Why?*
*Because, I wanted better for myself.*

I jumped into the fire,
ashes to ashes
I will rise again.

> **I declare victory over my life,**
> **and freedom over my fears.**
>
> **I claim abundance in my life,**
> **and welcome prosperity.**
> **I am worthy.**

We are all co-creators;
create what you want,
claim it and agree it to be true.

It's time to dig your way out,
it's time to claim your victory,
it's time for you to see your,
strength, beauty, and purpose.
It's time for you to meet your higher self.

Be seen as confident,
be seen as courageous,
be seen as crazy,
be seen as your true authentic spiritual being!

### Time to take action

Dare to become an artist,
Dare to jump out of your comfort zone,
Dare to create your own masterpiece.
It's possible.

Grab that doorknob
and turn the handle.

---

*Step forward and walk into your destiny.*

---

You are ready!
You possess the keys to change!
You have the opportunity to change!
You have access to change!

Will you make an effort and turn the handle and push the door open?
*Or will you complain it is closed?*

**Do something,**
or do nothing

Your future depends on your actions, not anyone else's.
You can wait, or you can go through the door, and change.

# CHAPTER 36

## *Feel empowered, not powerless*

> *"Life is a teacher,*
> *Some people fail,*
> *because they choose not to learn"*
> *-Giovanna*

This chapter, this book was written to you,
let's get some happiness passed around!
Order another round on the house.

There are;
words that can hurt people,
words that can break people,
words that can lie to people,
and words that defeat people.

But there are also words that hear people,
words that feel and understand people
and through written and spoken words can heal people.

Pay attention to the words you speak,
And breathe life and healing into others
xoxo
Giovanna

Law of attraction
is literally speaking things into existence.

> If we listened to what you said,
> of course, you would know what to expect.

> We create our own reality,
> want a raise, or a new job?
> Speak it into existence.

I've done it, and so can you.

Instead, of complaining about how much you don't like it,
or how it is so hard to find,
speak into existence, a job that you love, and a boss that appreciates you!

> Want people to respect you,
> start respecting yourself.
> The world is yours,
> God exists within us,
> feel empowered,
> and stop feeling powerless.

*Let's do this, anyone who is reading this;*

Let's get addicted to becoming stronger and loving ourselves a little harder.
Let's go crazy, and commit to forgiving OURSELVES, for the BS that we did,
or even what someone else did to us.

---

*Take your power back, by releasing the pain attached to the lesson.*

---

**It's time to be a little selfish and love yourself.**

Don't hold back, hug yourself, dance with yourself,
free the freedom and liberation your own soul can give you,
and become filled with your own greatness!

> You are empowered and loved by the spirit, it is time we really
> started living that way!
> Let's do the happy dance, because today we are addicted to becoming
> stronger, and loving ourselves unconditionally!

I am different,
I don't fit the mold,
and I am ok with that,
opinions don't matter.

> *I am dancing in my darkness
> and finding my light.*

Self-love above all

**Dance in your powers!
Celebrate your beauty,
and embrace the divine being that you are!**

> *The universe
> gives and receives.
> You get what you give.*

*Notebook Time:*

*Now is the time to write your next 30 days out.*

*What do you want to see? How do you want to feel?*
*What do you want to do? Where do you see yourself?*
*Who do you want to be? How do you want to be seen?*

*Create your own vision board in your notebook and sign and date it.*
*Listing everything you want to see in your reality, big or small,*
*practice the art of manifesting.*
*Happiness? New job? Self-love? Weight loss? New Girlfriend or boyfriend?*
*Straight A's? A new car? A pay raise?*

*We can ask for anything, but when we ask,*
*Align yourself with what you want,*
*you can make a million lists, but if it doesn't get met with belief or action,*
*it may never show up.*

***The universe***
***gives and receives.***
***You get what you give.***

# CHAPTER 37

## *Do you really need eyes to see?*

> *"I never felt connected, until I disconnected, and reconnected."*
> *-Giovanna*

When you lift the veil, and dare to step inside,
you begin to see things clearer than ever before.

*Things don't have to change,*
*for you to see it differently.*

> *The answers are where the truth is,*
> *the truth is where growth happened.*
>
> *The growth happened when we let go.*
>
> *In letting go, wisdom was gained,*
> *courage was multiplied,*
> *and understanding was found.*

When, I allowed the universe to move through me,
when I gave myself permission to let go, be happy, and speak my truths,
My world expanded,
and I began to live,
with freedom and happiness.

> Men and women,
> receive this message;
> you're not being held back,
> you're being pushed forward.
> What you're seeking, is not behind you,
> it's in front of you.
> Follow your path to where your heart leads.

If, there are all different types of fish in the ocean, or any body of water.
Why would we think everyone is alike?

Different species, different habitats, different food sources, all a part
of the giant food chain.
These are hundreds of types of fish, and there are millions of animals;
that fly, walk, crawl, slither, and swim across this earth.

There are warm-blooded, and cold-blooded,
ones that are covered in feathers,
others are covered in scales, or fur.

**There is a bigger picture to it all, and a greater understanding.**

*Not everyone is like us,*
*in fact, that is the contrast that perfects this picture.*

*We should embrace the whole animal kingdom,*
*each as a teacher, and a student,*
*we cannot have one without the other.*

*Looking for help?*

*If you are seeking a teacher,*
*or someone or something to help you on this journey on earth,*

*We need to first remember to start by looking within,*
*call upon the Spirit, your higher self, and your own guides.*

*Allow the wisdom to flow out of you, through you and to you.*
*Sit with nature, become one, feel grounded in all of your lessons, and hardships,*
*sit, and witness the understanding you need.*

# CHAPTER 38

## *Stepping into your own purpose*

*"Don't let the fear of heights and going upside down,
stop you from getting on and enjoying the ride."
-Giovanna*

Stepping into purpose,
can be very scary,
but it is also an amazing adventure,
rolled up in one giant life-size roller coaster.

The ride is filled with a much-needed adrenaline rush,
and we must learn to hold on tight.

>I am on a mission,
>the ride of THIS LIFETIME,
>to aid in world healing.

Yes!
You have survived!
You made it!

>Celebrate even the little victories,
>You did it,
>No one else, YOU DID!

Let your vibe speak for you,
you've got this.

Say it,
I've got this,
I've survived.
I know my strength now,
and I no longer fear the future.
Because of my past,
I know I can do anything!
I am greater than my past, and any mistakes!

*Conquer your fear of heights,*
*fastening your seatbelts,*
*And enjoy the ride.*

A message that needs to be shared,
we are confused with what makes us weak, and what gives us strength.

---

*It takes great strength to be gentle and kind.*
*Share compassion today*

---

# CHAPTER 39

## *Affirm your greatness*

> *"I am open and receiving to all that feeds my soul,
> and nourishes my spirit."*
> *-Giovanna*

You are worthy,
you are more than enough,

you need to see yourself,
as the amazing spirit that you are,
under the trauma, pain, setback, heartache, and defeats.

Now is the time to,
see your worth when you look in the mirror,
see your worth and value in your employment.

**It's time to love yourself and accept nothing less.**

**Heal within,
by going within.**

**Claim your greatness,
by defeating yourself.**

**Go after your dreams,
and let go of your fears.**

*Hold on get ready,*
**Rain is about to come.**

*Can you feel it?*
**Let it wash away your worries**

---

*Dance in the rain,
it's raining blessings!*

---

It's the beginning to your soul's abundance,
claim your happiness, and success.

We all deserve and are worthy of happiness.
Go within, and see what is reflecting outward,
tweak, check, and repeat.

We are co-creators,
we can, we will, we are able.

Speak life, and share life,

Speak abundance and share unexpected blessings with others.
Give more, than you seek.
There is no lack in the world,
abundance surrounds us all,
call upon it.

You are loved,
You are worthy,
You are strong,
You are able,
Speak it,
Feel it,
Dance, embrace, and embody.
You are the divine,
We are all connected,
Wake up soul sisters, and brothers!

Use your power today,
Use your power tomorrow,
Use your power
every day of your life.

Now is not the time to be timid,
Now is not the time to be fearful,
Now is the time to step up and be your authentic higher self!

**You are a manifestor,**
**You are an alchemist,**
**You are a magician,**
**You are a healer**
**You are needed**
**Here on earth.**

*Step into your light,*
*Step into your purpose,*
*use your gifts,*
*share them with the world.*

*You are here, on divine timing.*

I am here for the collective,
I am here to change the world,
one soul at a time.

Through my own healing,
I'm learning to heal others, my vibe is contagious,
and my purpose is expanding.

**We are all loved,**
**we are all supported,**
**We are all the divine.**

I am possible.

Speak what you want into existence,
Spread your passion,
Step into your purpose.

No one is holding you back, but your ego, and self.
Stay in peace,
Live with love.

*Notebook time:*

*Now that you have had some time reading, growing, learning, and facing your T.R.U.T.H.S,*
*it is time to write out fresh affirmations.*

*How do you see yourself?*
*Has it changed any since you first started reading this book?*
*Do you feel empowered?*
*Have you noticed your self-talk change? Are you catching your negative self-thinking?*

*Make a goal to start a gratitude journal*
*Each day write 5 things you already have in your life that you are grateful for and write 5 things you are grateful to see show up in your life. Do this before you go to bed, and the first thing when you wake up in the morning.*

*Let's continue to change your future,*
*one affirmation at a time.*

# CHAPTER 40

## *Confirmation of payment*

> *"When action meets purpose,*
> *the universe will pick up the tab."*
> *-Giovanna*

You've made it
you've survived through your worst day,
and you alive.

Step into alignment,
and claim your glory.

Spirit squad is celebrating,
Angels are rejoicing,
God is smiling.

We are protected,
We are guided,
we are here for a reason.

**Let go of fear,**
**and live.**

*If you were looking for a sign, here it is!*

**If you have been debating,**
**here's the answers.**

If you were doubting, *stop it.*
If you were questioning *don't.*

You've come this far,
you've lived this long.

There are no mistakes,
feel the joy,
feel the comfort,
feel the protection.

Dance, let go,

Give gratitude and thanks.
You made it!
You leveled up!

Go with your greatness,
Don't stop,
Keep going.

*You are all you need,*
*you've already got it all.*
*We are filled with spirit,*
*we are filled with power,*
*it's time to use it.*

---

*Now, is not the time to be timid, become overjoyed.*

---

This is what you wanted!
This is what you have been looking for,
**Confirmation**
For all your struggles, heartache, and pain.

Share this,
Spread the good news.

**You are well able,**
**you have leveled up,**
**you are healed,**
**you have risen!**
**You are powerful!**
**You are possible!**

**Speak greatness, into existence,**
**Speak life, over your life, health, family, work, and happiness.**

*This is a confirmation!*

*Confirmation of love and peace,*
*Confirmation of manifestation and beauty,*
*Confirmation of light and darkness,*
*Confirmation all is well,*
*Confirmation for your promotion,*
*Confirmation we are all guided,*
*Confirmation to step into purpose,*
*Dance in your own alignment,*
*Celebrate your own glory,*
*Share your light,*
*Live your story,*
*Heal your wounds,*
*Heal the world,*
*Give peace and gratitude.*
*There is competition,*
*but with self and ego.*
*We are love,*
*We are peace,*
*we are healing,*
*We are all doctors,*
*we are all healers,*
*We are all healed.*
*Believe and accept,*
*Receive and claim,*
*Speak victory,*
*Speak life,*
*Share spirit,*
*Share compassion,*
*Share your passion,*
*Share your purpose,*
*The time is now!*
*No longer can you hide,*
*You are protected,*
*There is nothing to fear,*
*Now is the time to be you!*
*-with love*
*Giovanna*

# CHAPTER 41

## *Flipbook the process*

> *"Most of the time growth is uncomfortable,*
> *which is why, most people don't grow.*
> *But to grow out of discomfort,*
> *is to finally realize your true beauty."*
> *-Giovanna*

This chapter is a combination of multiple quotes I wrote during my expeditions of life. It is a fusion of random life quotes, that I have written, that have helped me find my empowerment and embrace my growth.

---

Collected, and presented, to you on these pages,
in hopes of reaching your soul when you need it the most.
May the quotes appear, as the questions come.

---

Unlock your true potential,
you hold the key to wisdom,
it just requires silencing the ego and mind.

It begins and ends in the mind,
from there, it all changes outwardly.
You must want change,
or you'll drive yourself crazy
trying to resist it.

Retrograde,
currently purging my old self.
Healing broken parts,
letting go of the pain,
releasing anger,
forgiving the past,
renewing my soul,
and cleansing my spirit.

I have grown so much as a byproduct result of my greatest teachers,

my life lessons.
They were the ones that hurt me the most,
but they also propelled me
to become the beast,
I am today
Thank you.

2018 Mercury retrograde is here,
cleansing the soul and spirit of us all.
*Have faith in the universe and yourself,*
*You are more than able to survive in this life,*
*You are here to speak your truths.*

Share your gifts, shine bright, and be confident.
Feel the happiness, and freedom,
that releasing self-hate and fear can bring.

**The universe is whispering it's ok,**
**it's time to let go of those deep pains,**
**and unresolved relationships.**

It's time to release the self-hate and learn self-love.
It's time to let go of regret, anger, frustration, and hate!

**It's time we took control of our destiny and let our spirit free.**
**It wants to fly, and you were born with wings.**

I am, meeting myself face to face.
The struggle has been legit,
my self-destruction is real.
The confusion is finally, leaving,
the self-hate is slowly fading,
the fear is fake it always has been,
the love is real,
I am realigning.

The universe will take care of all,
we must learn to trust in the unseen God,
the universal provider of source.
The people who hurt you, will have their own time of learning.

Now is your time for a rebirth, growth and abundance,
but the only way is to make room!
Let go, let it be, and you will be free.
You have no limits,
but the limits,
we put on ourselves.

It's time to step into your own peace,
but you must let go, and leave behind all that has hurt you,
*all who have lied, or mistreated you,*
Karma will meet up with them.
*It's time you to meet up with your destiny.*
Your path is wide open,
you just need to make the first step.
You've got this love!

Yes, receive and accept this!
Affirm and declare,
I deserve the best,
I deserve to treat myself like the goddess I am.
I deserve to feel amazing,
It's not selfish, to care for yourself.

*Why were we taught that?*

When you take care of yourself,
you are then able to help those around you.
*Just like on an airplane,
you put your air mask on first,
before saving the person next to you.*

Use the salt water to cleanse your spirit,
There is something so beautiful in going through the process,
and then seeing the phases transform.

There is something so amazing and purifying to be cleansed by the ocean.
Feel the self-purity, and clarity wash over you as the salt water hits your skin. You are being showered with the very essence of bliss and happiness.
Soak up all the freedom, abundance, and wisdom within the vast infinite sea.

I am a beautiful soul in the unknown,
enjoying the process of Mother Nature cleansing my very soul.

I've learned that when we learn to enjoy every moment,
and we get excited in expectation of being immersed in healing waves,
then we can be cleansed, or go through a life-altering experience,
where we can observe it now as a cleansing process,
rather than traumatic drowning experience.

A lot of the time we are programed to understand and
see these experiences as setback,
but, that pain, that awful thing you lived through,
was really meant for our good.
It was meant for our growth, our healing, our cleansing,
and our expansion.

*Let us enjoy every part of the process.*

The downloads, and insight have been amazing,
ups downs, and face to face with my ugly truth.
Like a laxative to cleanses myself,
I drank up.

Almost, as if I were healing a leaky gut,
no matter our background or education,

**We have the ability, and responsibility
to take care of our mind, body, and soul.**

*There are tools in front of us, within us,
and available, to aid in our healing through the inside out!*

**The only way to truly heal,
is by getting to the root of the DI-SEASE.**

*I'll be right there with you.*

We are all connected,
either a reflection, or a lesson.

Instead of dismissing others,
learn to look at their soul and find the lesson.

In everyone we meet,
we are being taught something.

It might be patience at the light,
love for yourself, respect for a co-worker,
growth, and understanding
or maybe it's how to learn to speak up or walk away.

There is infinite knowledge,
surrounding us all.
You just need to be open to receiving the information.
Otherwise, you go through life,
mad, angry, resentful, fearful and confused.
Not realizing the people and lessons,
were only trying to strengthen your spirit, not break it.

**Next time you come across a situation,
instead, of saying why me?**

**Switch your thought process,
and ask how is this helping me evolve?**

What am I being taught,
or is this a repeat lesson?

*Am I supposed to react differently?*

Start to ask yourself questions,
and pay attention to the answers you receive.

*It's like constantly looking at life with 3d glasses,
and suddenly taking them off for the first time.
Realizing not everything is necessarily popping out at you,
it was only the vision you saw.*

You can't be bitter and expect your life to be sweet.
Stay hydrated and focus on yourself,
give yourself the love you crave,
satisfy your thirst,
and remain grateful for all that you do have.

I've learned a lot about myself, and others,
I celebrate my growth.

But I cheer and make a toast to my setbacks,
and to the people who are no longer in my life.

It was you that multiplied my strength,
Thank you!

To, the ones who hated me the most, and the majority who never
got to know me.

To, the situations that made me cry out, and the question can I survive this?!

To, the nights I wanted to hurt myself, because of the words of others
and the hate for myself.

*I am not perfect,
but I do know I'm pretty unique and amazing,
and so are you my love,
believe it!*

I am strong, determined, resilient, and above all loving, and kind.
I am a mixture of masculine and feminine,
although this is the first, I've embraced both at once.

*I've searched my whole life trying to find who I was;
the whole time too scared to look in the mirror.*

I am here on earth for a purpose,
and my journey has brought me through a lot,
but the purpose of my pain, was compassion,
understanding, and knowledge,
I see this now.
I've witnessed the divine connection between my setbacks and setups.

**I can no longer sit back feeling powerless,
scared, timid, fearful, or doubtful,
when I understand the truth behind it.**

*I've sat in the darkness,
and I now see the beauty in it.*

I've witnessed the clarity in the stars,
and felt the purifying essence of the moon.

Sitting in that total darkness,
I was embraced by the glow of the moon and brought back to life.

The best part,
the light that I possess, I am no longer scared to let it shine.

I encourage everyone to enjoy their setbacks.

*Do you know what comes after?*

Evolution increase growth, and alignment.

*I am still evolving,
but I am finally, aligned.*

**Speak what you want to see in existence:**

*I am a world-renowned published author, successful business owner,
and motivation speaker.
I am a healer aiding in the healing of the world.
I am a world traveler and philanthropist.
I will leave behind more than just words.
I will empower and uplift millions of men and women of all ages,
all across the world for years and generations to come.*

*Together, self and soul healing will occur,
and success and belief in self,
will develop.*

*Whatever you go after,*
*know that you are able,*
*and you have the power to do so.*

---

*I show my scars, and insecurities,*
*to help others see, we are more alike, than different.*

We are here to help and encourage each other,
All divinely connected,
here to teach us lessons.
Embrace it all!

Affirmation:

I embrace life and all that the universe offers.
I welcome change and healing.

---

*I wash away the past mental images of myself,*
*and embrace the reflection I now see in the mirror.*

---

My whole being is being transformed,
my fears are being seized.

My mask is being taken off,
my soul is healing.

My purpose is undeniable,
my power is finally, being accepted.

I have a gift,
We all have gifts,

Now is the time to share it.

The world needs your gifts!
Welcome yourself as a whole,
feel the warmth of your own embrace,
and the peace and comfort of your beating heart.

# CHAPTER 42

## *Messages to my soul tribe*

> *"It's time, to listen to the voice,*
> *your voice within."*
> *-Giovanna*

**Let the healing begin,**
**cue the dramatic angelic music**
**It is time get excited!**

Many have already started,
the greats have led the way,
I feel it in my soul,
the healing, and expansion,
is here to stay.

    It's time to use each of our own individual gifts, to heal the world.
    In our own unique way,
    using our own unique talents,
    telling our own unique story.

*Our pain is wisdom,*
*our knowledge,*
*is our purpose.*

    We went through it,
    so that we may be able to understand,
    relate, and have compassion.

    Re-learning we can heal ourselves,
    and share our healing with others, in our own individual way.

    This is a collective healing,
    Spreading wisdom, comfort, love, and guidance.

This is the time,
we've all chosen to be here, long ago.
Wake up precious,
it's time to get to work.

*Fear is false, it is fake,*
*you are made up of stardust, you can do anything.*

*This message is to everyone who has been wondering,*
*what to do,*
*what is their purpose,*
*what is happening?*


There is a shift, an awakening, a celebration, a healing taking place.
All you have to do is silence your mind and be present in the moment.
Allow spirit to move through you,
guiding you through every chapter of your life.
You do not need to know what to do,
you only need to know what not to do,
and that is loose faith and hope.


I used to be afraid of my own darkness.
Pure transparency,
I used to be scared of meditation.
As if knowing, already what I would be tapping into.

I was scared of my own powers,
which is why I want to empower others.

We need to understand our power, and start using it in our favor,
rather than against our own life, happiness, and health.
This life we have been blessed with, is filled with ups and downs,
success, and failure, but it was never meant to break you.
It was meant to empower you!

This year 2018
I've been owning up to my true purpose, and potential,
letting go, and releasing the doubts of losing people,
and fears of how they would receive me.

I'm still learning, we all are.
Life is a learning experience, it's our classroom.
No one's perfect.
*I can't help but share these messages I've received during my growth*
*ascension and descension.*

I feel like they are meant to be shared,
as well as confirmation for me.

Everything is going to be ok,
this is all a phase and a process,
of witnessing we are so much bigger,
than we ever imagined.

The lights not out for good!
**It's time to silence your mind
and allow yourself a face to face look at your reflection.**

Love yourself,
honor God,
honor your soul,
your spirit,
your potential,
and your power.

Own up and face your inner demons,
see what has been holding you back for years.

**Commonly, your greatest enemy is yourself.**

So please pass it on,
and thank you to all these amazing souls that help me on my journey.

I've taken many years away from social media in my 20's and came back
utilizing it for my growth, and expansion rather than my defeat
and mental setbacks.

*I appreciate you all so much,
you inspire and help in my healing, growth and renewal!*

We are all going through our own battles;
we have our own demons we fight with daily.
It's very easy to lose all hope and want to give up,
all because we choose not to fix it or address the core issue.

*There is no one identical to you,
you are unique,
but you're not alone.*

*There is still hope,
there is still compassion in this world,
I am sending out love and light, to you.
May you feel empowered and lifted up by it!*

There is so much self-hate, jealousy, envy
and pure disgusting HATRED in the world.

*I wanted to share my life,
in hopes to light another candle within,
all we need is one to light up any room.*

> **If you pass your healing on,
> imagine the places we can light up.
> Imagine the differences we can make
> by facing our demons.**

When was the last time you looked up?
Expand your vision and direction of thinking.
Have you noticed the galaxies above?
Star children are uniting.

> *Sometimes, life creates a pain,
> that we cannot run from.*
>
> *Doing it purely out of love,
> and our need for healing,
> growth and divine intervention.*
>
> *Listen to your intuition and receive,
> the answers given to you.
> Your questions are answered, by going all within.*

It's time,
to allow the healing to begin.
It's time,
to learn to speak your truths.
If you can't find your voice,
use your special talents, and gifts, to express your feelings and emotions.
Use your pain as a muse,
and create your own Mona Lisa.

> I am so moved by the tribe I've met so far,
> it's been a divine connection all across the world.
> I am grateful for all of the souls that have helped me along my journey,
> and for the connections we have created.

We are all interconnected.
Our stories, our pain, it is all connected.

---

*When you truly accept your purpose, your peace will follow.*

---

*I am so grateful and blessed,*
*I see myself,*
*my true authentic self.*
*After connecting with like minds and free spirits,*
*I've found it a little easier, being me,*
*My raw, authentic one of a kind true self.*

# CHAPTER 43

## Notes to self

> "I keep reminding myself my setbacks, are setups,
> remain calm have patience and show gratitude for change."
> -Giovanna

We are soon coming to an end of this book, the time that we have shared has been so divine and such a blessing.
As I write this, I can feel my spirit connecting with your mind.
I appreciate, and I am grateful for your purchase of this book and for taking time to read and take in my words that I have written.
A divine connection has been created and I look forward to meeting you personally, in the future, for some more Soul on Soul Contact.
This chapter is a collection of writings that have helped me through my own darkness, may it help you with yours as well.

I dare you, sweet precious soul,
to take off your mask,
let go of your chains,
and share your light with the world!

---

*My note to self*

*Let go of who they said you were,
and become who you want to be!*

---

*I am an ancient soul,
Assisting this planet in a human body,
We all have our gifts,
We all have our purpose,
No greater no less,
together woven by the divine for the good of mankind*
-Giovanna

          The sun,
       is not afraid to shine,
   even through the clouds she is noticed.
      If she were scared to come out,
   we would be living in complete darkness.

Don't be afraid to be like the sun,
shining bright and rising up in the sky every day.
Realize that just like the sun,
you are needed in this world.

I've found spirit in everything,
I don't have to go to a building,
or read a book to hear his voice.
Spirit speaks clearly to me, in all that I see and do, he is guiding me.
Every day is a blessing
a gift, and a teacher.
Tap in and here spirit,
there is no password required.

           As I grow,
        I learn, to let things go.
        Perfection and chaos
        I've been both of these,
        depending on the day.

But I'm getting better each day,
at keeping my peace and connecting.
Things that were once scrambled and mixed up,
are more clearly understood

Day by day, month by month, year by year,
a change here, a change there.
*"Ok, I understand this, change this, I don't know this, I am learning this."*
*Rotate, and flip this thought, rearrange, rethink and then reevaluate.*

It literally started clicking as I was going through the process,
and then boom, the answers start appearing,
as if I had broken the cryptic translation,

        *Take a deep breath and learn to go within,*
                *inhale, and exhale.*
        *Learn to call upon spirit, angels, and your ancestors,*
        *for your answers, guidance, healing, and protection.*

**You've got this, I've got this,
We've got this!**

Do you see the signs?
Spelling it out, we've got you.

### Calm down, relax and be still.

We confuse things like disaster, and chaos, with setback, and misfortune.
We let pain stop us from our own personal freedom and neglect ourselves.
We don't believe in our own abilities, *or do we not yet realize we have any?*

Yes, it is uncomfortable,
it can feel terrible at times, and not pretty,
But cleaning up waste isn't really fun.

If, we don't slow down and breathe,
and remind ourselves that we've got this,
we can feel like things are going out of control.

---

*Remind yourself,
you gain control, by giving up control.*

---

We are either prepared, or we will learn and get prepared.
No matter what you've got this!
You can see it as a win or lose,
or just allow it to be part of your practice.

---

*It's your own game,
the only way to win, is if you play.*

---

                **Let's face this beast,**
                   **whatever it is.**

                **A reminder to everyone,**
              **tell yourself you got this,**
           **and believe it, because you do.**
         **I believe in you, and so does spirit.**

You are in this to win it,
You may lose the battle,
but, continue to get up
and defeat the war.

             *"It's never been the destination,*
        *The strength is gained during the journey"*
                       *-Giovanna*

# CHAPTER 44

## *Quick tips*

> *"By facing your own T.R.U.T.H.S,*
> *you will be able to find healing, gain self-empowerment*
> *and*
> *through experiencing your vulnerability,*
> *you will find your own personal freedom."*
> *-Giovanna*

In this chapter you will find a few quick tips, and some repeats to help you, as you travel on your journey inward.

Don't forget to look up,
it's the perfect reminder,
that there are no limits.

---

*We create our own limitations,*
*The ceiling is only an illusion*
*-Giovanna*

---

I want you to know,
you make a difference in this world
You are truly amazing and appreciated.
You have accomplished and helped more people than you can imagine,
you are closer to your victory than you realize!

**Don't give up and pass on the hope!**
**Death can also mean rebirth.**

One of my keys to my growth and expansion,
is I love and welcome change.

**When change is happening,**
**growth is occurring**
**and success is being planted.**

I know all is well,
keep your balance,
and ride the wave.

*Some people don't want you to heal,*
*because they can't heal themselves,*
*they also don't want you happy,*
*because they have lost their source of happiness.*

*What are you going to do?*
*That is ok, keep on healing.*

It's always been about you,
don't get distracted.
Focus on your own lane,
perfect your own life, and get it done.

**Be the best,**
**let go of the rest.**
**Abundance is here for us all,**
**put in the effort and reap the reward.**
**There is no way around success,**
**you must earn it.**

*I learned to dance in my darkness,*
*and capture my own light.*

We are all radiant beings of the divine,
all we need to do is silence the mind,
and go within.

---

*Sometimes, all we need to do is detach, to reattach.*

---

**self-growth is healing,**
**link backup with self.**

Recharge and refocus daily if not weekly

Try it today,
it is leveling up time.
Take control over your life, your happiness, and your peace.
by letting go.
*We are all teachers, and we are all students.*

>Know your worth and don't feel guilty for not giving discounts.
>If you're priceless, not everyone can afford you.
>There will be people envious and jealous of you,
>it has nothing to do with you.
>Stay humbled, love yourself and create your own happiness.

Time to clean up and release,
it's just like taking out the trash.
You've got to continually, and repeatedly,
take out the trash,
but it keeps your house clean.

>Don't be lazy,
>quit making excuses,
>take control of your actions.

Let me explain,
after losing myself to others,
after breaking and continuing to break,
I am starting to find my freedom and liberation.
I found my purpose in speaking my truths,
I am starting to feel lighter and lighter every day.
I have learned to give myself freedom,
I'm finding myself a little more,
I'm learning to say no,
I'm learning to rest,
I'm learning to love myself,
and I'm learning about myself.
I appreciate my journey,
and I appreciate the people I've met on my travels so far during this lifetime

>*I can finally, say I know I'm on the right path.*
>*Inward*

It's time,
there's a shift,
I feel it, can you?
Nature is our teacher,
showing us the beauty in
death and rebirth.
Demonstrating there is life and lessons in all,

It's time we started to get less distracted, and more focused,
It's time to do less blaming, and more forgiving of self.
It's time to let go of the pain you've been carrying,

let go of the heartache,
let go of it all,
for personal freedom.

You do not have to justify the pain,
You do not have to justify the anger,
but now is the time to let it go down the steam,
let it become purified and washed away by the flowing water.

> You don't have to keep fighting a war that was meant never to be fought.
> Put down the sword
> Put down the knife
> It's ok you are safe
> You are protected

> Once we allow ourselves to let go of all the past emotions,
> we can allow ourselves to release
> that baggage that we've been holding on to.

---

*This next destination your headed to,*
*requires no baggage just bring yourself!*

---

I've been working on slowing down,
and taking time away, to speak with nature.
Finding my grandmother willow all around.

> A gentle reminder,
> we are all connected,
> living in their world together.

Animals in nature never worry about where they will find nourishment
or shelter, they just know deep within they will be ok.
They haven't lost that ancient program, every generation reborn with it.
They know there are predictors and they also know they are prey.

Eat and be eaten is all connected.
All things live, all things die,
this is the cycle of life.

All for a greater purpose,
they do not live any differently,
knowing one day they may get eaten,
they also do not worry about the past or future

they truly live in the present.
Knowing all is well.

*Wise ones who walked the earth before us,*
*thank you for showing us the magic*
*through living your authentic life.*
*Your gifts changed the world.*

*All things are connected,*
*and all stages are combined,*
*threaded by the great divine, providing for all.*

*You're worth the forgiveness you seek,*
*Give it to yourself.*

*When it all comes together, and you realize you were never crazy,*
*just enlightened*
*11:11*

# CHAPTER 45

## It's never goodbye it's only, see you later

*"This journey that we are on, is truly amazing, when you think about it,
and we are never alone.
But, just like anything, you have the option
to see it two ways,
as punishment, or enlightenment,
as a setback, or a set up.
You decide, you have the power,
feel empowered."*
-Giovanna

Precious souls,

I hope you felt the intimate soul on soul connection.
I cannot describe the joy this book brings me, for so many reasons,
and as I read this through one last time,
I apologies for any grammar errors, this was self-published with
very little help.

Writing this final section, I feel empowered.
Empowered for writing my truths out and
taking the first step inward, letting go,
but also taking control of my life.
With a brand-new ancient upgrade of thinking,
it has caused my life and my health to become transformed!

I feel empowered for sharing it with you,
I know this will be received many ways,
for everyone is at a different level of perception.

*I found my inner courage and received help from above,
to finally, complete this chapter of my life.*

With months of hesitation,
once this is published it is for the world to see.

Off to reach millions of people,
off to make a difference,
off to be a ray of sunshine

a beacon of hope,
in someone's life.
I had to write to you, this wasn't an option anymore, this is just the
beginning. As I complete this first book, you can just now start to see
the border come together of this life size puzzle spirit has me putting
together. There is the entire inside of the puzzle that will
eventually be revealed.

**Spirit and the universe will be directing my steps,
one by one,
to align the correct pieces perfectly together in Divine timing.
Only spirit has seen the completed puzzle, he created it,
I follow eagerly with faith.**

I finally, had the faith to believe in myself,
to believe this almost ridiculous dream spirit put in my head many year ago.

It was so big,
it scared me.

*This book Soul on Soul Contact,
was written and completed well over three times, one after
the other, sharing totally different depths to my soul,
and way different approaches,
until I found the perfect blend.*

This is the first of many, this is only the beginning,
this is much bigger than me.

**I am a vessel, a messenger, a student, a guide,
a healer, a teacher, a mother of nations.**

The constant whispers telling me to continue,
as much as I wanted to ignore, and stay hidden,
I was necessary.

The divine coincidence to save a life, help or heal a soul,
and change their perception of how they see themselves, and the world.

**This book may highlight me,
but it bleeds for humanity.**

Do you feel the connection?
Did you hear the calling?
11:11

**My growth and healing took a huge leap when I took control of my thoughts.**

I am excited to share with you, connect
and unite as we proceed on our own adventures.
I know my life was meant to be shared,
to connect to many souls,
on different levels, and understandings.

My target reader and desired audience was you.
The exact person reading this book.

Written to the universe,
for the universe
delivered
to you.

It must have been coincidence.

This will reach many souls,
and hundreds of countries,
one by one aiding in healing.

You asked,
the angels delivered,
me to you.

We are all messengers of spirit, all gifts of hope.

When we open and expand,
release and let go,
we can allow,
and grow.

*Do you know what happens when you allow and grow?*

Change happens,
miracles, and unexpected blessings occur,
healing, financial change, your entire outlook and life transforms.

You witness firsthand the abundance surrounding you.
In every area of your life, love, finances, opportunities,
and best of all, self.

I know it is not always the cool thing to change what you listen to,
or the group of friends you hang out with.

                **Remember and become empowered,**
                    **You have the power to change.**
            **Choose yourself, and your own priorities,**
        **you decide if you want to grow or remain stagnant,**
                    **based on your mind's environment.**

Start a change in your own group of friends, have a manifest party,
where you all get together and talk about your dreams and create a game plan. Helping and holding each other accountable,
connecting and vibing on a whole other level.
Soul on soul connection,
a Sign of Empowerment.

                **Take charge, or be taken, mentally.**

*Change your mentality,*
*and you will change,*
*your outcome.*

                    **The key to remember,**
            **is you and I are not being punished,**
                      **just the opposite,**
          **we are being planted, with love and care.**

Spirit may allow us a season of drought,
to starve out and allow parts of us to die.

There may be seasons of hardship,
in order to grow our spirit muscles.

There may be seasons of storms,
knowing ahead of time, that you will need the rain to grow.

And we may even grow with weeds,
knowing they will be picked up by the roots, once fully grown.

        **We must be gentle on yourself, you still think your only human,**
            **but day by day enlightenment will call out to us,**
                **all you have to do is pick up,**

Do not rush to give up,
do not become fearful, or doubtful.
Just the opposite,

                        **Get excited!**
                    **Get encouraged!**
                        **Get ready!**

**It is** time,
it is **your time,**
to become who you are, under all of those protective layers.

Raw and unfiltered
soul on soul
what do you want out of life?

*Who are you and who do you want to become?*
*What do you see when you dream at night?*

That dream will soon be a reality,
If you begin to believe.

**"For me,**
**my journey was taught to me**
**through**
**Self-sacrifice."**
**-Giovanna**

I was taken down the road of the unknown,
scared out of my mind.

*Only, once I let go,*
*could I finally, be let in.*

*Magically, my doubt,*
*was replaced,*
*with many lifetimes of faith.*

**It is amazing how the universe uses us as messengers,**
**divine intervention, at perfect timing.**

I understand and feel your deeper purpose here on earth,
it is greater than the present troubles of today.
I've been reuniting and working with others,
To remind us who we are.
Becoming a sign of empowerment.

**Knowledge is meant to be passed on.**

Just like running a marathon,
towards the end, your legs are numb, and you feel like you are floating.
You are exhausted and in pain,

Keep going through the motions,
keep feeling the emotions.
You are getting closer to the finish line,
and after you complete this marathon,
training for the next race.

*It is never ending,*
*but use your skills to work for you,*
*rather than against you.*

Your strong will is resilience use it!
Your pain is strength, find it!

Give gratitude, affirm your greatness, and have confidence your world will align.

The time you missed, will be made up.
Don't give up, give praise and witness the glory.

**You are spirits walking testimony,**
**Put a smile on it.**

Use your spotlight to continue to share your story, insight,
lessons, faith, and understanding.

That crazy vision you have of sharing your unique story,
and helping others or using your talents,
will come true one day.
If, you keep pushing forward,
and step into the unknown.


Affirm, the destiny you want to see.

Your journey has humbled your ego,
and your battles have tamed your demons.
You are now on the other side.

Open your eyes
and soak in your victories.
Can you feel the light?
Can you hear the angelic celebration?

You have been looking for signs and confirmations,
You are it!
You are the sign for others and yourself.
The confirmation that you not only survived,
but are thriving!

**It is your time!
You've been in the darkness wondering when….?
It is now!**

*I don't know what your question was.
But concerning timing, the answer is NOW!
Everything you need, you already have.
Now is the time to start, they will help you along the way.*

We are here to overcome our differences together.
Our journey may be taken alone,
but your help, and talents, are needed everywhere.

With your healing, it will multiple like a ripple effect.
Share your light,
share your gifts,
write your story.

**Your pain is a priceless tool that you have been gifted with,
use it to create a masterpiece just like you.**

You know your strength deep down, do not be scared to show it off.
Just because others are intimidated, does not mean you must hide in
the darkness.
It is time to grow from the ashes
of those who once burned you!

I've recently created a safe space on Facebook, a group called
Signs of Empowerment, as a follow up and meeting place for all that have read this book. A place where we can chat and explore your own truths. If you feel the urge to continue growing and finding your empowerment with me,
I ask you to join, this is your personal, invitation.

You can also add/follow me on Instagram
@Iam.possible212
@signsofempowerment

I look forward to connecting and hearing how this book has impacted you,
and I am so excited to read about your T.R.U.T.H.S

By healing ourselves, it is a ripple effect toward world healing.

I will talk to you soon
With love,
   Xoxo

*Giovanna*

www.ingramcontent.com/pod-product-compliance
Lightning Source LLC
Chambersburg PA
CBHW020356170426
43200CB00005B/194